Gulbahar Haitiwaji
Rozenn Morgat

HOW I SURVIVED
A CHINESE
'RE-EDUCATION'
CAMP

Translated by
Edward Gauvin

First published by Canbury Press 2022,
by arrangement with Editions des Equateurs, Paris, France.
This edition published 2022

Canbury Press
Kingston upon Thames, Surrey, United Kingdom
www.canburypress.com

Printed and bound in Great Britain
Typeset in Avenir and Kolkorn by Canbury Press
Cover: Alice Marwick

This is a work of non-fiction

ISBN
Hardback: 978-1-912454-90-7
Ebook: 978-1-912454-91-4

Gulbahar Haitiwaji
Rozenn Morgat

HOW I SURVIVED A CHINESE 'RE-EDUCATION' CAMP

Xinjiang is a desert region in north-western China.

'THROUGH VOCATIONAL TRAINING', MOST TRAINEES HAVE
BEEN ABLE TO REFLECT ON THEIR MISTAKES AND SEE
CLEARLY THE ESSENCE AND HARM OF TERRORISM AND
RELIGIOUS EXTREMISM. THEY HAVE NOTABLY ENHANCED
NATIONAL CONSCIOUSNESS, CIVIL AWARENESS,
AWARENESS OF THE RULE OF LAW AND THE SENSE OF
COMMUNITY OF THE CHINESE NATION.
THEY HAVE ALSO BEEN ABLE TO BETTER TELL RIGHT FROM
WRONG AND RESIST THE INFILTRATION OF EXTREMIST
THOUGHT... THEY ARE CONFIDENT ABOUT THE FUTURE.'[2]

'NOT ANY FORCE CAN STOP XINJIANG FROM MOVING
TOWARDS STABILITY, DEVELOPMENT AND PROSPERITY.'[3]

1. Referring to the Chinese 're-education' camps in Xinjiang

2. Excerpt from an interview given by Shohrat Zakir, Chairman of the Xinjiang
Uyghur Autonomous Region and the Communist deputy party chief of Xinjiang,
to state media (Xinhua News Agency), 16th October 2018

3. Shohrat Zakir, Chairman of the Xinjiang Uyghur Autonomous Region, during
a press conference on Xinjiang held by the State Council Information Office in
Beijing, 9th December 2019

To all those who didn't make it out.

To Fanny, Gaétane, and Lucile – free women.

Preface

Gulbahar survived internment. She endured hundreds of hours of interrogation, torture, malnutrition, police violence, and brainwashing. On the basis of a photo of her daughter taken during a Uyghur diaspora demonstration in Paris, China sentenced Gulbahar to seven years in a re-education camp. Her trial did not take place until after a year in detention. It lasted nine minutes. Neither a judge nor lawyers were present. Gulbahar stood all alone in the dock, facing three police officers. For a long time, she was sure she would be executed. Then she was overcome by another certainty: she would die in a Xinjiang prison camp. No one – not France, where she had lived in exile for the last decade, nor her daughters and husband, Gulhumar, Gulnigar, and Kerim, all three of them political asylees – would be able to rescue her. All around her, she had felt the trap that China had set closing around her, once and for all.

Deep in her heart, Gulbahar was riven by conflict: should she go public and tell the world her story, or remain in the shadows to protect her loved ones? During our conversations in her apartment, she seemed cautious, resigned to keeping her true identity a secret.

Gulbahar was born into a Uyghur family that had lived in Xinjiang for generations. Like her ancestors, she was raised in that oil-rich land of deserts and oases, for centuries troubled by deep-seated geopolitical conflicts that had, apart from brief bursts of independence, resulted in long periods of Chinese annexation. The arrival of the Communists in 1955 led to the province becoming part of the People's Republic of China and being renamed the 'Xinjiang Autonomous Region.' Since then, this vast territory, more than six times the size of the United Kingdom, has suffered from colonisation at the hands of China's ethnic majority, the Hans. Over time, oil refineries developed, Chinese tractors paved the way for sprawling cities, and Communist red overran the land with countless banners, flags, and paper lanterns. From minor intrusions to large-scale discrimination, Uyghurs were subjected to the first manifestations of what is now clearly full-scale genocide. One day in May 2006, exhausted from seeing their prospects for the future fade before their very eyes, Gulbahar and her family left to start a new life in France.

Because Uyghurs are Sunni Muslims and their culture is Turkic rather than Chinese – and because China was late in absorbing them – their (minority) separatist fringe flies the sky-blue flag of East Turkestan. In 2009, the Ürümqi riots, which claimed the lives of several hundred Hans and Uyghurs, were met with unprecedentedly violent repression. The authorities had an impressive arsenal of weapons for surveillance and control: armies of cameras that used facial recognition, police on every street corner, and from 2017 onwards, 'transformation-through-education' camps. The region became the most highly surveilled place in the world. As a gateway to central Asia, it has also become a centrepiece of Xi Jinping's 'New Silk Road,' or Belt and Road Initiative. Bordering eight countries, Xinjiang is a strategic linchpin for this colossal infrastructure project, aimed at connecting China to Europe.

To date, Amnesty International and the Human Rights Watch estimate that more than one million Uyghurs have been sent to, or are interned in, camps which China persists in designating as 'schools,' where teachers claim to 'eradicate Islamist terrorism' from Uyghur minds.

Gulbahar has never had the slightest interest in her country's politics. She admits as much with a hint of pride: when she speaks of her religion, she speaks of a 'peaceful' Islam, a 'moderate' Islam. She is neither a separatist nor an Islamist terrorist. And yet she was sent to a camp. Herein lies the hypocrisy and perversity of the Chinese concentration camp system, which seeks not to punish an extremist Uyghur minority, but instead to eradicate an entire ethnicity, right down to those of its members living in exile abroad, like Gulbahar.

✳ ✳ ✳

One morning in November 2016, Gulbahar received a mysterious phone call from Xinjiang. An employee of her former company was requesting that she return to China. For 'administrative formalities,' he specified, 'documents concerning your forthcoming pension.' Gulbahar was wary, but not wary enough. A few days later, she landed in Ürümqi, and her ordeal began. Authorities confiscated her passport, threw her in jail, and then, after months in a cell without trial, she was taken to a camp.

In the camps, the 're-education' process applies the same remorseless method to destroying all its victims. It starts out by stripping you of your individuality. It takes away your name, your clothes, your hair. There is nothing now to distinguish you from anyone else. Then the process takes over your body by subjecting it to a hellish routine: being forced to repeatedly recite the glories of the Communist Party for eleven hours a day in a windowless classroom. Falter, and you are punished. So you keep on saying the same things over and over again until you can't feel, can't think anymore. You lose all sense of time. First the hours, then the days.

❀ ❀ ❀

In the living room of her apartment in Boulogne on the French coast, with her daughter on one side and myself on the other, Gulbahar relived these moments of pure emptiness. She would concentrate, frowning slightly, her face sombre. What had she felt when guards chained her to her bed for 20 days? 'Nothing,' she'd reply with the worried air of someone brooding on the strangeness of their own answer. When she was forced into a truck one icy December night with no idea where she was going, Gulbahar thought she'd be shot in the middle of the snowy desert. And what had she felt then? Nothing, either. 'At the time, I was already dead inside.'

And when she was told she was free to go? 'I stayed there on my bed, my back to the guard.'

Over the course of her 're-education', her human emotions had deserted her. The intimacy of our conversations helped her to recover them. As her daughter Gulhumar – the driving force behind her release and our interpreter – looked on, deeply moved, Gulbahar acted out every scene of her ordeal. Her voice became the police chief's, low and loud, or took on the persecuting tones of the fake judge who'd passed her sentence. When words failed her, she'd get up from the sofa to show us the hobble of shackled ankles, or the upright march of military processions. Stiffly, she paraded around the living room, arms pressed straight to her sides. She would pivot toward us, then break out in a telling laugh. 'Absurd, right?' We'd all laugh. By making fun of herself and those she'd met, she was exposing the madness of the concentration camp system.

When recounting the confessions she'd made under police duress, Gulbahar was overcome by an uncontrollable fit of hysterical laughter. In fact, mockery and its attendant laughter often freed her from her trauma.

But the experience of the camps cannot be healed so quickly.

In addition to her lasting physical repercussions, Gulbahar remains a haunted woman to this day. Haunted by the thought that China, despite freeing her after difficult negotiations with the French Foreign Ministry, might come knocking at her mother's door, or those of her friends and siblings who stayed behind in Xinjiang. By denouncing the Chinese Communist Party loud and clear, she could summon police violence as swift as thunder upon her loved ones. Like her, they could be interrogated, imprisoned, tortured, deported. Like her, they could be treated as 'criminals' and 'terrorists.' Like her, they could be swallowed whole by the camps, losing their dignity as human beings and their happy memories, too (any memories, in fact), and then, gradually, their desire to live. That was not something she wanted. Anything but that.

One morning in September 2020, sitting on the white sofa of her apartment, Gulbahar devoured the introduction to this book. It had been just over a year after her release, her arrival at Charles de Gaulle airport, her reunion with Kerim, Gulhumar, and Gulnigar. As she read, her old idea of revealing her true identity in the book came back to her. 'She hasn't said anything yet, but she's thinking about it,' her daughter told me. A few days later, she came to a decision. 'This is my story. I want to take responsibility for it. It is my duty as a Uyghur,' she declared. She was taking a huge risk. No one who reads this book will be able to deny that.

China is far from halting its concentration camps in Xinjiang. To date, neither the UN nor any other international delegation has been able to see for themselves the scope of the genocide. As China continues to imprison Uyghurs in camps and sterilise women of Uyghur ethnicity, Gulbahar Haitiwaji speaks on their behalf in this book. We owe a debt of gratitude to her and her daughter, Gulhumar.

Rozenn Morgat

Contents

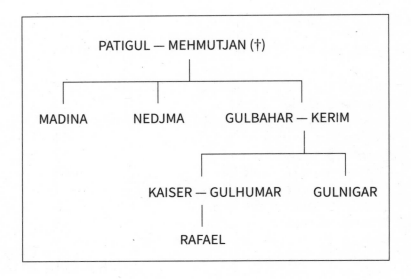

Gulbahar's family tree

1. A Family Wedding

That night, in the stifling heat of late August, a splendid party was under way. Under the spotlights, laughter mingled with the clink of dishes, a boisterous symphony playing over the melodies of lutes. Alongside mauve table runners laden with roses, guests flocked to multi-coloured vermicelli, great steaming tajines, and baskets of *samsas*, pastries stuffed with ground meat and onion.

At Uyghur weddings, the dancing never stops. Nor, for that matter, the eating. Anything less would be missing out. All night, music drowned out the conversations. People got up from the tables to shake their hips, then sat right back down again to guzzle a bowl of *polo*[1] or drink a cup of tea.

---

1. *A common Uyghur dish of lamb sautéed with rice, diced carrots, and onions.*

Never before had my cooking so utterly delighted my guests. They were all so stylish, stuffed into dark suits and shimmering dresses. In China, the Han people claim that Uyghur women are the most beautiful in the world. That night, when the women laughed, their teeth flashed in the dark; their eyes, accentuated by a stroke of eyeliner, widened over high cheekbones. One of them was shining more brightly than the rest: Gulhumar, the bride. My daughter. You should've seen her, corseted into her dress of tulle and white satin. A string of fine pearls around her waist showed off her graceful curves. Her rich, dark hair, swept up, bared the back of her neck and her round, upright shoulders; an elaborate bustier cleaved snugly to her breast and lower back. Oh, the grief that dress had given us! I can still see Gulhumar sulking in the dressing room mirror, fists on her hips. Frills and sequins had never been her thing. As a child, she'd dreamed of being a boy. It was the source of all her drama, her obsession, her pipe dream. She'd do her best to join in any activity that might bring her closer to her goal. Nothing could stand in her way. Not dresses, not leather shoes, not ribbons in her hair.

The reception was a smash. Long after, guests would whisper that Gulhumar's wedding had been wonderful. In the Netherlands, Norway, Sweden... wherever Uyghurs in exile on the continent had found refuge, the bride's beauty was extolled. Such kind compliments helped my husband Kerim and me almost forget those who had been noticeably absent from the gathering: family members who had stayed behind in Xinjiang. Xinjiang is where this story begins: the story of our family, the Haitiwajis, but also my own story.

❀ ❀ ❀

My name is Gulbahar and I was born in Ghulja, in Xinjiang, on 24th December 1966.

Before France took us in, we were living in a wondrous land of plenty. Almost nothing of it is left now. Our people there have suffered relentless repression for decades. We Uyghurs have been and continue to be persecuted, locked up, 're-educated.'

But let's start at the beginning. Xinjiang is thousands of miles from France, at the edge of Central Asia. Kerim and I grew up in a paradise as big as some entire countries, dotted with mountains and oases. This jewel is located at the far western end of China, surrounded by eight neighbouring nations: Mongolia, Russia, Kazakhstan, Kyrgyzstan, Tajikistan, Afghanistan, Pakistan, and India. Its riches include gold, diamonds, and citrus fruit, but also other resources underground: natural gas, uranium, and – above all – oil. I say 'our land,' but that's not exactly correct. This land, serried with independent republics to the west, has known only sporadic, fleeting stretches of national independence between long periods of Chinese annexation: first under the Empire, then with the arrival of the Communists in 1949, who named it 'Xinjiang' ('Xinjiang' means 'new frontier' in Mandarin). The uprisings of separatists dreaming of an independent Republic of East Turkestan came to nothing; the communists paved over our gravel roads with cement and gutted the bowels of the earth to get the oil and gas there.

Since then, we Uyghurs have been the pebble in the Middle Kingdom's shoe. Xinjiang is far too rich a strategic corridor for China to lose. China has invested too much money in the 'Silk Road

Economic Belt,' an epic political and economic project intended to join China to Europe via Central Asia. Our region is a crucial link in this project. Without it, the ambitious goals of the policies China's President, Xi Jinping, is spearheading would never see the light of day. He needs Xinjiang: a docile Xinjiang conducive to commerce, cleansed of separatist populations and sectarian tensions. In short, Xi Jinping wants a Xinjiang without Uyghurs.

In schools across China, students recite that the 56 national ethnicities – of which Uyghurs are one – are the cornerstone of China's cultural influence throughout the world. On our government-issued identity cards, it says that we are citizens of the People's Republic of China. But in our hearts, we are always Uyghurs. We pray to God in mosques, not Buddhist temples. The most devout Muslims have beards, and their wives go about veiled. In the homes, schools, and streets of Xinjiang can be heard the rough, husky intonations of the Uyghur language, a dialect derived from Turkish. Our staple food is not rice, as it is among the Hans to the east, but rather naan, a round flat bread found across Central Asia. And yet, more than ever in today's context, our cultural differences are a source of disturbance and our past revolts a cause for worry. That is why some of us fled to France in 2006 – just before Xinjiang was subjected to unprecedented repression.

When we arrived in France, few people had ever heard of Xinjiang, much less the ethnic and cultural conflict raging there. When we spoke of discrimination, detainment, how impossible it was to build a peaceful future there, the reaction was a raised eyebrow. Usually, our explanations were met with indifference or at best, polite curiosity. 'A bit like with Tibet?' we often heard. Sure, a bit. To Westerners, there was something exotic about the repression we were undergoing. It was like a Chinese version of David and Goliath. Except in this version, David still hasn't won. He's been fighting the giant for generations, to no avail. In truth, I couldn't put my finger on the exact moment the troubles began in Xinjiang. They were already there, hiding in the shadows, when I was growing up in my northern village. Perhaps they've always been there.

Still, for Kerim and me, everything got off to a good start. There had been a time not so long before when Xinjiang's political problems barely touched us. Its distant music reached our ears, but we were too busy building a life for ourselves. This was in the 1990s. Xinjiang was attracting everyone who wanted to make a fortune, from China and beyond. Its capital, Ürümqi, swarmed with newly graduated engineering students. Han families emigrated from the east, Kazakh labourers come to work small plots of land. Downtown, office towers and malls shot up, some taller than the mosques. Oil companies were hiring right and left, Uyghurs and Hans alike. The Grand Bazaar played host to a motley crowd: women in veils beside those in blue jeans and hoodies, mothers with their children riding sidesaddle on the backseats of scooters, bearded fathers in embroidered doppas, the traditional Uyghur skullcap. Amid concerts of blaring horns, vendors squatted on the sidewalks with their electronic wares, plastic toys, and costume jewellery that the Chinese from the east couldn't get enough of, while right beside them, stacked in large plastic bins, lay wooden cooking implements, henna, and naan.

Kerim and I met on the benches of the Petroleum Engineering School at Xinjiang University. Ürümqi has a special charm, accommodating people from all over, with their own diverse cultures and traditions. Hans make up almost half the population. The other half is divided among a multitude of ethnic minorities: Uyghurs, Kyrgyzs, Kazakhs, Tadjiks, Mongols... Kerim came from Altay, a far northern city at the feet of the mountains that form the border with Kazakhstan, Russia, and Mongolia. Its bronze-skinned inhabitants had a reputation as uncouth mountain people who spoke a dialect derived from Kazakh rather than Turkish. At first I didn't see the charm of this strapping, thickset lad. I was from Ghulja, a small town, also in the north. Back then, getting there from Altay meant travelling several hundred miles through the empty desert by bus or car. A whole world lay between us.

I remember our neighbour in Ghulja. A short, stocky woman who lived with her husband, who was just as short and stocky. Just why they lived there escaped me; all we knew about them was that they were Han. But the wife dressed in traditional Uyghur clothes. She made samosas stuffed with mutton and lamb skewers whose aroma filled our little alley. Han or Uyghur, it didn't matter back then. At least to us. We had a wonderful relationship with our neighbours – the woman and her husband even shared our Eid feast. She treasured our culture. It was hers too.

After that we moved to Karamay, the other major city of the north, whose name means 'black oil' in Uyghur. This concrete city was thrown up to house the families of hundreds of workers come for the nearby oil fields and was said to be an El Dorado.

On graduating, the local oil company there offered us jobs as engineers. When we arrived there in 1988, there was nothing to see but a grid of empty streets modelled on American cities – no shops, restaurants, or even a bazaar. On every block were building sites with a din of jackhammers, cranes, and diggers. You woke and went to sleep amid a cacophony. The city screeched, creaked, and rumbled nonstop. Towers sprouted from the ground in a matter of weeks to welcome new families of workers from all four corners of Xinjiang. While they were filling up the city, other workers were busy digging a course for a man-made river and planting rows of luxuriant trees along it. At the centre of this hive of activity, we lived in a small one-bedroom apartment supplied by the company and adjacent to its buildings. We stayed there for over two decades, and in all that time, the construction never stopped, as if Karamay kept spreading over the earth full of black gold.

We led a frugal life. We would freeze in winters. In January, the temperature hovered dangerously around -30 degrees Celsius (-22°F). A brutal wind howled through the streets, stinging people's faces. As soon as spring came, it was sweltering. In nights in May, the paving stones gave off a stifling heat after baking all day in the sun. While families returned to the cool of their apartments to dine, we would make our way through the torrid soup on Kerim's bike: him on the seat, me on the rack with my arms around his waist. The city was new, like our life together. We were making it up as we went along. The future was bright and lay before us. We were married in the privacy of our apartment with an imam and a handful of friends to celebrate. Then the girls were born and the future truly seemed more radiant than ever.

Our income was just enough to scrape by each month, but we had few needs. It was a time of simple pleasures. Our friends – some from Ürümqi like ourselves and others we'd met through the company – also led modest lifestyles. Everyone worked long hours. At the office, the weeks flew by, each much like the next. To provide some relief from the job, we instituted a tradition: at the start of every year, we'd all write down our names on little scraps of paper and put them in a big bowl. Every month, we'd pick out a name to organise an outing for everyone: a restaurant, a sauna, a party at someone's apartment. These gatherings were a breath of fresh air. Karamay grew; entertainment options multiplied. What wonderful times we had, everyone sitting together over grilled meat skewers or just we women, laughing as we lay in a Turkish bath on a girls' day out! If one of us was short on funds one year, we'd all pitch in to help out. We'd all left our hometowns behind to work in this new city in the middle of the desert. By dint of growing up far from our families, we'd made a new family here: Ali, Nilopar, Muhammad, Dilnur, Aynur... I wonder what became of them. No one in that group left Karamay. Last I heard, some were still working for the company, others as elementary school teachers or college professors. These days, we hear from each other less and less often, as if our friends fear someone might be spying on their confidences. No Uyghur who stayed in Xinjiang escapes the eye of Chinese Big Brother. I wouldn't want my questions to cause them trouble.

I think Kerim always knew we'd have to leave Xinjiang. The idea had taken root in his mind long before we were hired by the company. It went back to the years in Ürümqi when we'd just graduated and were both looking for work. This was in 1988. We pored over the wanted ads in the papers. In many of them, the following words could be made out in fine print: 'No Uyghurs.' That always stayed with him. The rising wind of discrimination followed us all the way to Karamay, blowing ever harder, but at the time, we all preferred to look the other way. Except Kerim. Kerim wasn't buying it. While I refused to dwell on such details, for him it became an obsession.

At the company, the *hong bao* were the first incident. Hong bao are red envelopes containing money, given out to loved ones during Chinese New Year. Traditionally, employers also distributed these to their workforce. Our boss at the company never missed an instalment. But one year, word got around that Han employees received more money than their Uyghur colleagues. Uyghur families did not dwell on this episode. After all, maybe it was just a rumour. But shortly thereafter, all Uyghur employees had their offices transferred to the edge of town. A handful among us objected. I didn't dare; I put my things in a box, and a Han moved into my office at company headquarters. A few months later, Kerim applied internally for a promotion. He had all the required qualifications and the seniority. There was no reason not to choose him. But the position was given to someone else. A Han employee who didn't even have an engineering degree. Such coincidences multiplied. Our daughters grew older. Kerim grew discontented.

As for me, even comfortably ensconced in denial as I was, I saw our prospects for a future here dwindling. Disappointments at the company had slowly eaten away at Kerim. In 2002, he left

Xinjiang to look for work abroad. He went to Kazakhstan first and came back after a year, somewhat sceptical. Norway was next. Then France, where he applied for asylum. He settled down there; the girls and I were to join him once he'd obtained refugee status and found a job. All our friends said he was crazy, starting over from scratch like that. Especially since, by all appearances, life was smiling on us in Xinjiang. Over the years, Kerim and I had seen our salaries improve. After Gulhumar was born, the company had furnished us with a more spacious apartment in the centre of town. The girls were pursuing a promising education in Uyghur schools. We had a nice car. In short, we were now part of a certain elite, and so I mostly agreed with our friends. Moreover, I'd never left my province. The thought of being plonked down in some other part of this enormous world filled me with anxiety.

How much humiliation, inequality, injustice does it take before someone rises up and cries, 'Enough!'? According to a Chinese proverb, anything can happen to anyone at any time.

In Xinjiang, checkpoints, police inspections, interrogations, intimidation, and threats were so common we barely paid them any mind. So it was that we lived on borrowed time, in a state of partial freedom that could be snatched away from us at any moment. Being invited over for tea at the neighbourhood precinct was part of our daily lives. We'd tell the police about our day, give them the names of our friends and acquaintances, talk about what was going on at work. This was the price of relative tranquillity.

The more total surveillance becomes, the more it becomes part of daily life. All Uyghurs had a brother, a friend, a cousin, a nephew who'd had trouble with the police, if not disappeared for a couple of months. Yes indeed, anything could happen. To anyone. Each citizen was a potential dissident. And in each Uyghur family, centuries of cultural rebellion lay dormant, which made us all dissidents from birth.

This conflict had begun long before the Communist annexation. So why get all heated up over a little more discrimination?

Like other countries in Europe, France is made up of a multitude of cities, villages, and hamlets full of dwellings, businesses, and cafés, themselves full of human beings. There are people everywhere. In Xinjiang, 400km (250 miles) of bare earth lie between the two largest cities in the north, Ürümqi and Karamay. Outside of these urban centres, built near oases and oil fields, silence and solitude stretch as far as the eye can see. Barrenness stifles any sign of human life. The rows of jagged mountain peaks afford the only relief from the unbroken line of sky and desert. It couldn't be easier for the local secret services to arrange for a dissident to disappear and bury his body in the middle of nowhere. Being a Uyghur in China means living with this knowledge in the pit of your stomach: that at any moment, you might disappear into the vast desert of Taklamakan.

This is also why I've always kept my distance from political matters. As a child in Ghulja, I grew up without ever hearing my parents complain about the government. They worked in a nearby distillery, where they did their best so that the eight of us, their children, lacked for nothing despite their meagre wages. I think they were more preoccupied with our survival than any discrimination aimed at Uyghurs. We were a humble family, living far away from the big cities where ethnicities mingled.

As I grew older, I became a shy and studious young woman. At university in Ürümqi, I steered clear of the political issues that laced our conversations. I didn't know enough about them to say anything, and all this activist anger frightened me. But it suffused the atmosphere in the capital. When I met Kerim, a whole new world opened up to me. Kerim was all about politics. He could talk about it for hours. His eye would light up when a conversation threatened to turn into a debate. All around us, students from the four corners of the land were stirring up new ideas. Everywhere, the crushing weight of the Cultural Revolution was crumbling. In Beijing, hundreds of thousands of students had occupied Tiananmen Square for weeks in 1989 to demand democratic reforms from the government. People weren't yet talking about what had happened there, but our student movement was a lot like it.

Out of love and perhaps a little curiosity, I went with Kerim to the demonstrations in Ürümqi in 1985. We were demanding more social equality for ethnic minorities, an end to the one-child policy, and that the Communist Party grant our province political autonomy. Our movement, like all the others, was nipped in the bud, thankfully without bloodshed. The police silenced our leaders, and the rest of us returned to our classrooms at the university without getting our way. But the fire burning inside Kerim never went out.

One night in the year 2000, he came home without a word. He'd had time to mull over his disappointment at not getting the executive position he'd applied for, and now it had come to a head: he'd made his decision. I looked at him, and I saw the same rebellious spark that used to light up his eyes. 'I resigned,' he said simply, dropping a box with the company logo on it in the living room. I was ready to explode. Then he said, 'I've had enough.' Deep down, I knew he was right.

On the night of our daughter's wedding, as Gulhumar was giving out hugs to the last guests, the same thought crossed my mind once more: Kerim had been right. I was surer than ever now. France had given us back our freedom. At the same time, in Xinjiang, a new wave of terror, more violent than ever before, was crashing down on the Uyghurs.

That August in 2016, a month of so much joy for us personally, saw the arrival of a new player on the Xinjiang scene, one crucial to the power struggle between our ethnicity and the Communist Party: Chen Quanguo, Secretary of Tibet from 2011 to 2016, known for having instituted draconian surveillance methods there. He was appointed Secretary of Xinjiang. Under him, the repression of Uyghurs took on a tragic scope. Thousands were sent to 'schools' hastily built in the middle of the desert. In reality, these were internment camps where detainees were subjected to brainwashing – and worse. Only a few ever came back, and those that did returned broken.

But at the time, with the dance floor bathed in a soft orange glow, the last guests wrapping their shawls around their golden shoulders, and car engines purring in the courtyard outside, the horrors that Xinjiang was witnessing were still unknown to me. I was light years away from imagining that a few months later, I'd be plunged into the maelstrom of these events. There was nothing but Gulhumar, her white dress, and the warm glow of happiness in my heart.

2. China Calling

19th November 2016
Paris

The man on the phone said he worked for the oil company: 'Accounting, actually.' His voice was unfamiliar to me. At first, I couldn't make sense of what he was calling about. He mentioned my unpaid leave, which had begun when we left Xinjiang in 2006. There was static on the line; I had a hard time hearing him. 'You must come back to Karamay to sign documents in order to receive your pension, Madame Haitiwaji,' he added.

'In that case, I'd like to grant power of attorney,' I said. 'A friend of mine in Karamay takes care of my administrative affairs. Why should I come back for some paperwork? Why go all that way for such a trifle? Why now?'

The man had no answers for me. He simply said he would call me back in two days after looking into the possibility of granting power of attorney.

It had been years since I'd heard from the company. The urgency in the man's voice, which I'd found unpleasant, took me back a decade. As I drifted through my kitchen in Boulogne, I saw the broad building of ochre stone once more. The courtyard that you could only see once you were through the security checkpoint, past the automatic gate that lifted like a salute from a sentry. I tried to picture this man from accounting: he must have been short, his face swallowed by a pair of rectangular lenses, his body by a rolling desk chair. On the phone, in the background, I could hear the air conditioning breathing down his neck and his secretary's fingers tapping frantically away on the computer keyboard. The office they shared must've been cramped, poorly ventilated, covered in yellowing wallpaper peeling at the corners.

Oh, how I'd loved that place. I'd even wound up loving my job. Once I'd dreamed of being a doctor or a nurse. When I finished high school, I'd applied to all the medical courses in Xinjiang, but my test scores weren't high enough. I was sent to Xinjiang University in Ürümqi to become a petroleum engineer. I got used to maths and mechanics. Like medical students performing a dissection, we cut open many a machine and studied its innards, from the electrical systems to the gearbox. I wasn't the best student, but I got by. What I liked the best was imagining plans for refineries. Like an architect, on big sheets of drafting paper, I'd pencil out the maze of a site with its complexities of piping, cranes, and pumps. Every month our professor would post the four best plans on the classroom wall. Mine was always one of them. It was my pride and joy.

Then Kerim and I were sent to Karamay. At the time, the pay was good, and made up for the company's gruelling working conditions. The idea of sweating away in the desert amid the din of cranes didn't especially appeal to me, but rules were rules: new recruits had to spend a year onsite at a refinery. I'll never forget, as long as I live, all the pipeline segments, ends gaping, stacked like lumber in a yard against the sides of hangars. The nonstop ballet of machines hanging from above, their razor jaws hauling still-glowing pipes from the furnace. The screech and burnt smell of welding, sutures the labourers administered to the ends of the pipes in a spray of bluish sparks.

The year after, to my great relief, the company relocated me to the headquarters in Karamay instead of one of the extraction sites outside town. There, I was entrusted with a unit for production safety. As before, I got used to a trade I had never learned and wound up liking it. Years went by, I moved up through the company and came to feel grateful towards it. Despite discrimination against Uyghurs, the company paid Kerim and me decent salaries, enough to raise our daughters without wanting for anything.

But in 2002, Kerim left. Without him, life became an exhausting exercise in walking a tightrope. The weeks were like tunnels I dived into head down, no time to think. I juggled work, the girls, chores, and phone calls with Kerim. I was worried sick over him, as he wandered the streets of Paris, waiting for his asylum paperwork to go through. He slept in a homeless shelter when there was room, and made do as best he could when the shelters were all full, which happened a lot that winter. But, he told us, he'd get those papers. Soon, the icy nights spent waiting for dawn on a subway platform or a terminal at Charles de Gaulle airport would be distant memories, 'hassles' from the early days. A bit nightmarish, sure, but these were just the kinds of things you had to go through on a big adventure like this, he reassured us.

His bravery and perseverance have always fascinated me. They proved him right once again: Kerim found a job as a chauffeur. He was his own boss, with a company called Uber. Here he was, the former engineer from Xinjiang, the undocumented migrant who'd turned up in Paris without a name or an address to call on, now driving strangers around at night. His car sped down the brightly lit Champs-Elysées, the avenue that had made his jaw drop when he'd first arrived. It rattled over the cobblestones of Place de la Concorde and down the damp streets around Les Halles.

The months went by. Soon came the anniversary of his arrival in France. Despite uncertainties over his application, which was still being processed, his enthusiasm took the upper hand. He didn't talk much on the phone about his living conditions, which were rudimentary. He preferred to spin tales about the wonderful faraway land that would welcome us all as a family. He described the Eiffel Tower, a heap of scrap iron that reminded me a bit of the crooked cranes hanging over the oil refineries in Xinjiang; the tranquillity of tree-lined paths in the Luxembourg Gardens; spring sunlight bouncing off the picture windows of modern apartments while the river Seine ran by below; the cool morning air. Over time, he'd found a niche for himself. A few Uyghur families showered him with kindness. He was learning French.

Since Karamay, the girls had been following his adventures

as if he were a hero out of one of those American TV shows they watched after school. They had no idea how hard all this was on him. As for me, the prospect of joining him filled me with apprehension. When we left Xinjiang at last in 2006, I didn't have the heart to resign. Closing the book on the company seemed too difficult. Unlike Kerim, I hadn't been hurt by the company. Not yet. I took leave – unpaid, but extendable – so I could hold onto my position as an executive engineer. After all, maybe we'd come home someday. On 27th May, Gulhumar, Gulnigar, and I landed at Charles de Gaulle International Airport in Roissy.

The girls obtained refugee status, like their father. In seeking asylum, my husband Kerim had made a clean break with the past. Obtaining a French passport in effect stripped him of his Chinese nationality. For me, turning in my passport held a terrible implication: I would never be able to return to Xinjiang. How could I ever say goodbye to my roots, to the loved ones I'd left behind – my parents, my brothers and sisters, their children? I imagined my mother, growing old, dying alone in her house at the foot of the mountains. Giving up my Chinese nationality was giving up on her too. I couldn't bring myself to do it. So instead, I applied for a residence permit that was renewable every ten years.

As I looked around the quiet living room of our Boulogne apartment, my head was buzzing with questions. Why did that man want me back in Karamay? Was it a ploy so the police could interrogate me? Nothing like this had happened to any of the other Uyghurs I knew in France. All around me, the apartment in Boulogne was steeped in the lethargy of early afternoon. Kerim was the only other person home. Snug on the white couch, he was

35

scrolling through the latest news on his mobile phone. He was about to start his shift. Saturdays, requests would keep coming in until late at night. A ray of winter sun fell on the kitchen tiles. Only the muffled hum of the washing machine broke the silence. The day we'd walked into this apartment, there hadn't been a single stick of furniture, no curtains, no couch. Just a frying pan left out on the electric stovetop and Kerim, in the middle of the living room. Nowadays, the memory made us laugh. We still gently ribbed Kerim about his frying pan. Really, was it reasonable for me to go away for several weeks and leave Kerim alone with the girls?

❊❊❊

Two days later, the man from the company called back. 'Granting power of attorney will not be possible, Madame Haitiwaji. You must come to Karamay in person.' I gave in. After all, it was only a matter of a few documents.

'Fine. I'll be there as soon as I can,' I said.

When I hung up, a shiver ran down my spine. I dreaded going back to Xinjiang. Over the last two days, Kerim had been doing his best to reassure me, but I had a bad feeling. At this time of year, Karamay was a city in winter's brutal grip. Gusts of icy wind howled down the avenues; the shops, houses, and apartment buildings all huddled close together. A few bundled-up figures braved the elements, hugging the walls as they walked, but on the whole, there was not a soul to be seen outdoors. Truth to tell, though, the temperature was just a tiny part of why I was scared. All you had to do was Google 'Xinjiang' to see that security measures in the region were growing ever more extreme. An innocent person who set foot outside their home could be arrested at the drop of a hat. That wasn't new, but the despotism had become more pronounced since the Ürümqi riots in 2009.

In Xinjiang, the 5-8th July 2009 will forever be known as a dark time during which the delicate balance that still allowed Uyghurs to believe that a happy future awaited them was shattered. An explosion of unprecedented violence struck the neighbourhood around Xinjiang University in Ürümqi. Dozens of Uyghurs – hooded, clubs and knives in hand – devastated the area, assaulting residents, slashing, beating, and battering Uyghurs and Hans alike, leaving people unconscious in the streets. This is an important point: Uyghurs, too, were victims of this spike in extremist fervour. Later, the Chinese Communist Party would blame the entire ethnic group for these horrible acts, justifying its concentration-camp policies by claiming that Uyghur households were a hotbed of radical Islam and separatism.

Images that we were not allowed to see at the time paint a picture of unspeakable horror. Women with mangled faces and children in their arms run screaming past burning buses with broken windows. It's unclear if these children were dead or unconscious. Wracked with sobs, figures knelt before shattered shopfronts or beside motionless bodies.

The next day, the Hans retaliated. In the end, the total body count came to 197. Since then, a region already beset by brewing violence has sunk into chaos.

That summer, I'd gone back to Altay on my own for vacation. Almost 800km (500 miles) away from Ürümqi, I spent peaceful days with my in-laws. I thought of Kerim and my daughters, who hadn't been able to come with me because of their refugee status, as usual. Outside, big dark clouds crowned the mountain ridges.

News of the attacks reached us in dribs and drabs, like scattered raindrops before a storm. First a few sprinkles here and there. Then a deluge. All around us, neighbours claimed there were countless instigators. Others said that every night since the rioting began, Ürümqi had been plunged into darkness so that police could 'clean up' the city. Even that those who'd been unlucky enough to witness the events firsthand had been locked up or executed. At the same time, to almost total indifference, the internet had gone down. On TV, not a word was said on the subject of the unrest, arrests, and killings. Cooking shows and reportages on Xinjiang's famed oil-rich subsoil aired nonstop. But no one paid any attention. In our homes, fear had set in. After these riots, many Uyghurs fled to Europe and the United States.

In 2012, I realised that the country would bear the scars from these riots for a long while to come. It was summer vacation again. We had gone back to Xinjiang to visit our friends and families, as we did every year. But that year, the atmosphere weighed on us as soon as we landed. I went to my mother's in Ghulja, then to Kerim's family in Altay, and Karamay where our friends had stayed. The distances between each were tremendous, miles through desert without a living soul. Joyfully we rediscovered the austere, arid landscape: craters the wind had formed in the hills, where nothing grew; oases with their lush vegetation that hinted at the arm of a river or a nearby spring.

That year, I paid no attention to nature's beauty. The car my friends and I were driving in was stopped every 50km (30 miles) by roadblocks. Groups of five or six officers would ask us to stop, get out of the car, and show our papers while they inspected the truck, the doors, the glove compartment.... There had always been checkpoints in Xinjiang. But never this many.

Karamay looked like a city under siege. Groups of Han policemen strolled through the packed streets. You could pick them out from their uniforms or, if they were in plainclothes, by the small clusters they formed at intersections. In Xinjiang, you could never tell who was a policeman and who wasn't. They blended into the crowds. That year, I saw veiled women and bearded men asked to show their papers and their mobile phones. Once upon a time, police had invited suspects over for tea at the precinct. How many times had I watched Kerim head off after getting a text message from our local station? I shuddered at the thought of never seeing him again. But this time, the cops weren't going to all that trouble. They were just stopping people right in the street!

Now another four years had passed. I didn't want to go back. But Kerim was surely right: there was no reason to worry. The trip would only take a few weeks. 'They'll definitely pull you in for questioning, but don't panic. That's completely normal,' he reassured me. My life was in France now, and the police in Karamay knew it. They couldn't keep me. I silenced the voices whispering in my head. I ignored the increasingly bad feeling I had. I wanted to be done with all this as soon as possible. Be rid of this chore. I grabbed the iPad on the living room coffee table and browsed flights for Xinjiang. On that day, 21st November, 2016, I bought a round-trip ticket to Karamay: an outbound flight for 25th November, returning 11th December. The day I left, as Kerim unloaded my suitcases from the car, I squeezed my darling daughters tightly in my arms. We weren't used to public displays of affection in our family. They only happened on rare occasions, and I never knew quite what to say. We never cried much, except at weddings.

I was only going for two weeks, but feelings were running high. Seeking to soothe things, but also just because the thought happened to cross my mind, I said, 'I hope nothing happens to me!' Kerim grumbled something along the lines of 'What are you talking about?' Gulnigar gave me a smile. Gulhumar got upset and said she hoped I hadn't jinxed myself. She had no idea how right she would be.

3. A Police Interview

29th January 2017
Karamay

The cell door shut behind me. What time was it? Late, surely. It was night outside already, I'd caught a glimpse. Beneath the blinding fluorescent lights, bodies lay this way and that. In the cramped cell stood two guards asleep on their feet, eyes half-closed, facing the people strewn on the floor, who seemed to breathe as one. The two guards were wearing detainee's uniforms, but I wasn't paying much attention to them then. As I struggled with the shackles guards had put around my ankles, there was only one thing rattling around my head: 'This isn't over, Gulbahar Haitiwaji. It's only just beginning.' They'd worn me down. There were too many of them. No matter how I'd screamed and condemned their lies, it had done no good: I'd signed their damned sheet of paper where I confessed to having participated in 'conspiring to stir up trouble.' And now, I was lost.

The cold and the smell were unbearable. When the police brought me here, I caught a glimpse of the sign over the gate that led to these huts: 'Karamay County Jail.' I was in police custody, the waiting room for prison. I didn't know why or for how long. No one would answer my questions. No one told me a thing. When they'd confiscated my passport a month ago, Kerim had reassured me over the phone: 'There's nothing they can do to you. Your family's in France. They have no right to hold you for no reason. Don't worry.'

But I should start from the beginning. It all began with the company, a few days after I arrived. It was 30th November. That morning, I'd gone in to sign the vaunted documents for my upcoming pension. In the office with its flaking walls sat the accountant, a sour-voiced Han, and his secretary, hunched behind a screen. Aynur, the friend I was staying with in Karamay, stood just outside the door, nervously twirling the fringe of her shawl around a finger.

In the car on the way over to the company, Aynur couldn't help voicing her opinion: 'But still, coming all this way for a few signatures... it's a bit unusual, isn't it?' I listened with one ear, both moved and distracted. I was glad to see her again. Out of the window, the landscape paraded past, just like I remembered it. She didn't want to worry me unduly. 'After all, there are so many things that make no sense in this country!' she finally said, to put an end to the discussion. Then she'd changed the subject to something lighter.

In the cramped office, I diligently paged through a stack of documents, on the lookout for any potential traps. I had just two pages left to initial when three men entered the room. They were tall Uyghurs in civilian clothes. Aynur stared at them, trembling. Her coppery complexion had gone green. They were police officers. But Kerim had said this would happen, so I wasn't worried. I'd been waiting for them. I recalled his comforting words: 'Remember, you're coming from France. As soon as you set foot on the ground, they'll know you're back for two weeks. They're bound to ask questions. Don't worry.' The policemen were not forthcoming about the reasons for my arrest. All they said was: 'We have some questions for you. It can't wait. You must come with us at once.' Next thing I knew, the biggest of the three was putting me in handcuffs. I repeated Kerim's words of wisdom to Aynur: 'Why are you afraid? Don't be afraid.' Before leaving the hallway, I gave her one last encouraging look. She nodded, her face still frozen. Later on, she told me she'd gone to the bathroom and thrown up.

The next part took place in the Kunlun police station in Karamay, a ten-minute drive from the company. On the way, I prepared my answers to the questions I was likely to be asked. I tried to steel myself. After leaving my belongings at the front desk, I was led to a soulless room: the interrogation room. I'd never been in one before. A table separated the policemen's two chairs from what was to be my own. The quiet hum of the heater, the poorly cleaned whiteboard and the pallid lighting set the scene.

We discussed the reasons I'd left for France, my jobs at a bakery and a cafeteria in La Défense. I thought I was prepared for anything, but the conversation was shaping up to be a game of ping pong. Back and forth went the ball: they asked, I answered.

The policemen were pleasant and wondered if France was as nice as people said, if I was happy there with my husband and children, if the food was good. One of them handed me a bottle of water. I turned him down. 'Not too tired?' he asked. Later, I'd grow leery of these tactics for lulling captives into comfortable conversation, but not this time. Not yet.

That was when one of the officers shoved a photo under my nose. It made my blood boil. I'd have recognised that face anywhere. Those full cheeks, that slender nose lost between them – I leaned closer. It was my daughter, Gulhumar. She was posing in front of the Place du Trocadéro in Paris, bundled up in her black coat, the one I'd given her. In the photo, she was smiling, a miniature East Turkestan flag in her hand. The occasion was one of the demonstrations organised by the French branch of the World Uyghur Congress to speak out against Chinese repression in Xinjiang.

Whether you're politically active or not, such gatherings in France are above all a chance for everyone to get together, much like birthdays, Eid, and the spring festival of Nowruz. You can attend to protest repression in Xinjiang, or also, as Gulhumar did, to see friends and rebuild some sense of the community we'd lost in leaving Xinjiang. At the time, Kerim was a frequent attendee. The girls went once or twice. I never did. Like I've said before, politics isn't my thing. I've never been interested, and since leaving Xinjiang, I'd become less so.

Suddenly, the officer slammed his fist on the table. 'You know her, don't you?'

'Yes. She's my daughter.'

'Your daughter's a terrorist!'

'No. I don't know why she was at that demonstration.'

I kept repeating, 'I don't know, I don't know what she was doing there, she wasn't doing anything wrong, I swear! My daughter is not a terrorist! Neither is my husband!' My memories grow muddled here. The rest of the interrogation is a blur. All I remember is that photo, their aggressive questions, and my futile replies. I don't know how long it went on for: half an hour? Four hours? I remember that when it was over, I said irritably: 'Can I go now? Are we done here?' Then one of them said: 'This isn't over, Gulbahar Haitiwaji. It's only just beginning.'

With a lump in my stomach, I recovered my belongings. Outside, it was almost dark. My phone showed several missed calls from Kerim. It was 5.30pm. He hadn't heard from me since 10 that morning. Seven whole hours without a word – an eternity in Xinjiang. I called Kerim, shivering. 'Where were you? I was so worried! Are you all right?'

I told him everything. The tears I'd been afraid to let show before the policemen came pouring down my face. Then, disoriented, eyes puffy, but somewhat heartened, I tottered back to Aynur's. 'Praise God, they let you go!' she cried, giving me a tight hug. I wasn't so sure. In a few hours, I'd become a hostage in my own country. Without my Chinese passport, there was no way I could leave Xinjiang. I was doomed to roam this place, dependent on developments in an investigation that would determine whether or not I could board my flight home on 11th December.

The days went by, subject to the ironclad and unbearable law of waiting. The officer who'd interrogated me phoned daily to monitor my movements. With his every call, my hopes of returning to France crumbled away a bit more. 'Certain items still require verification,' he said. 'You must wait,' or 'You must be patient,' he would add with insidious sadism. I crisscrossed Xinjiang like a lion in a cage, in search of a solution that was nowhere to be found: not at my mother's in Ghulja, not at Aynur's in Karamay. No one had any answers for me. Worse yet, discussing my passport problems with friends could land them in trouble as well. While dining out with them, I sometimes managed to slip a word or two to whoever was sitting next to me at the restaurant. 'The police are evil now,' they'd murmur amid the clamour of conversation. 'Yes, it's getting worse and worse. Poor you!' My loved ones were not short on bravery, but their replies, as disappointing as they were formal, made me realise the degree to which they too were hostages in this country. Apart from saying prayers and offering compassion, my friends and family were no help.

The weeks went by, and with them, I imagined bogus indictments piling up in the folder with my name on it on the desk at the precinct. Exhausted by all my running around, I slowly succumbed to that state of resilience normal for Uyghurs in Xinjiang. That is, until the eve of Chinese New Year. That day, the police officer called me for the nth time, and this time, his voice betrayed developments in the case. 'You must come back to Karamay at once. It's urgent.' I was seething, convinced he was trying to play another one of his tricks. 'I can't. I'm spending the holiday at my mother's,' I retorted. 'What if I said you could get your passport back?'

Now my blood was really boiling. The next day, I kissed my mother goodbye and hopped on the first flight to Karamay, filled with hope. How naïve I was. The police had no intention of returning my passport. This was but the latest tactic for crushing what little composure I had left. After a string of questions – always the same ones – followed by what I thought were administrative and medical formalities with a view to closing my case, they led me to the county jail in Karamay.

❀ ❀ ❀

Fifty days had passed since I had been due to return home. Back in Boulogne, Kerim, Gulhumar, and Gulnigar were worried sick. My family in Xinjiang were no longer answering the phone when they called. Nor were my friends. No one had seen me. Temperatures in Karamay kept falling perilously, reaching -30 degrees Celsius (-22°F). Then Kerim had an idea: why not contact intelligence agents in Xinjiang? They had access to my file. They must know where I was being kept. Kerim knew one. The man owed him a favour.

Back when we were still going to Xinjiang for summer breaks, Kerim's phone would ring the minute we unpacked our bags. He'd pick up – the number was unlisted – and on the other end, a man would introduce himself, offering neither his real name nor his job, but simply inviting Kerim over for tea in a room at a downtown hotel. Odd, as invitations went, but not for a Chinese person, much less a Uyghur, especially a political asylee like Kerim. Everyone in China knows what to expect when a police officer says, 'Come over for tea.' It's a summons to an interrogation. You don't say no. The man would then give Kerim the address of the hotel and hang up.

These interviews were not like the routine calls to the precinct. No, these men were actual domestic security agents. High-ranking intelligence agents so adept at the art of interrogation that they could go from a pleasant conversational tone to barbed coercion techniques in just a few seconds. Civil servants specially recruited to surveil our movements and the company we kept. 'What do you do with your days? What is your job? Are you in touch with Uyghurs there?' Then, abruptly: 'You do know that the World Uyghur Congress in France serves the interests of Rebiya Kadeer, don't you? That woman is a known terrorist. Do you take part in events sponsored by the Congress? Better keep your distance.' Kerim would dodge the issue. Behind the closed doors of the hotel room, he gave them enough information to satisfy them without revealing the truth of involvement with the World Uyghur Congress in France. Over time, he too had become adept at the art of being questioned.

These exchanges were always cordial, even amicable, in the end. But both parties knew just how far the tacit agreement between the two of them could be taken. If Kerim suddenly refused to comply with proceedings, they could make him disappear in the blink of an eye. He might've been thousands of miles from Xinjiang, but China still kept its eye on him. The Communist Party would never let him live in peace. 'You must remain at our disposal. Do not leave Xinjiang without notifying us. We may need to see you again. And try to say good things about China and Xi Jinping when you go back to France, all right?' After a few hours, Kerim would leave the room feeling drained but relieved.

Police are so ubiquitous in Xinjiang that despite the fear they inspire, relationships between officers and the citizens they interrogate sometimes take an ambiguous turn. Kerim always loudly proclaims: 'No, I never snitched on anyone.' He's proud of that fact. 'It was good tea, so I stayed,' he often says, a bit of humour to break uneasy silences. To him, those men were connections he couldn't give up, and that is why he still had one of their numbers on his phone. That day, consumed by fear that he'd never see me again, he decided to get back in touch with a certain police officer.

At the same time, in early 2017, Gulhumar was scrolling through her contacts. One of her friends worked at the Karamay propaganda department. Another had married a policeman in town. They should be able to glean an address, a name, a phone number. She reached out to them both. 'Don't worry, I know lots of people, especially policemen,' the first replied on WeChat. The second promised she'd convince her husband to look into it; the file must be somewhere in a database in a Karamay precinct.

Weeks passed. Gulhumar's follow-up messages went unanswered. Then, one day, she realised that her first friend in Karamay had, instead of helping her, cut her off and blocked her on WeChat. She wouldn't get anything more from her. 'Stop writing to us, my husband will get in trouble,' wrote the second friend. Gulhumar had run head-on into the impenetrable wall of silence. It was Kerim's turn next. 'You won't find anything about your wife. I couldn't access her file even if I tried,' his contact said sombrely. Kerim couldn't get over it. He blew up on the phone: 'How can that be? She must be somewhere! She hasn't vanished off the face of the earth!' The agent replied, 'You know that in Xinjiang things don't work like they do in the rest of the country.' He was currently in retirement far from Karamay. According to him, the files of people who were sent to the camps did not appear in the databases. Or else they were so well-hidden as to render them impossible to access. Even those who enjoyed cosy positions in the Xinjiang administration lived in fear.

Knowing the right people wasn't enough. Knowing me had become compromising, a potential prison offence. The mere fact of speaking with someone abroad could land you in hours of questioning. What happened to Kerim's agent and Gulhumar's two friends? Were they followed? Threatened? Interrogated? Accused of collaborating? Kerim and Gulhumar never found out. But one thing is certain: the agent was right. In Xinjiang, things didn't work like they did in the rest of China. Making someone disappear was well within the realm of possibility. Worse still, it was easy.

Gulhumar realised she couldn't count on anyone but herself. Gulnigar was too young. Kerim's French wasn't good enough to make their voices heard. The protests, the flag-waving by the Trocadéro, photos of the faces of detainees – none of that did any good. They aroused sympathy in onlookers, but not action. At any rate, Gulhumar had never liked protests. She also hated it when people thought of her as a 'poor little refugee.' She did everything she could to meet lawyers, politicians, reporters. Her goal? To make sure no one could ignore what had happened to me.

4. Communist Party Glories

30th January 2017

The buzzing refrain grew louder. As if someone were fiddling with the volume knob on a radio. Louder. Even louder still. The squawking was unbearable. No, not squawking – children shouting. Singing about the glories of the Communist Party. The aggressive rhythm of the patriotic hymn took hold of me as I opened one eye, still numb from the feverish sleep of the night before, my first night in jail. Like a boomerang returning to its owner, it all came back to wring my guts: the tears that wouldn't stop falling, a heart I couldn't feel beating anymore, a stomach that quailed beneath the weight of fear. And the horrible, dirty, too-thin leggings that my shackles kept me from rolling up over my ankles. How long had I been asleep? A few minutes? An hour? Who was the young brown-haired woman curled up against me?

My eyes lingered on the room's bare grey walls. Even the smallest squalid details leapt out at me beneath the piercing fluorescent lights that shone down mercilessly day and night. But already I could hear the footfalls of guards. The girls – nine of them – untangled themselves from grey blankets and lined themselves up empty-eyed on the edges of the beds, hands flattened on their thighs. Two Uyghurs and seven Hans. Our features were different. We weren't the same kind of people. Uyghurs are olive-skinned, almost bronze, with features that stay angular even with the rounding of age. Whereas Hans have the lighter colouring and thicker skin of eastern peoples. Their women are slender and lack the curves of Uyghurs. Their roots are Asiatic. Ours are Turkish.

I copied their motions while three people – a cook escorted by two guards – entered the room. The girls grabbed their bowls. I did the same. Hands held out a scrap of stale bread, and I heard the slop of a liquid being poured into my bowl. Greyish congee. I retched. My head spun. Was any of this even real?

Among the girls, I recognised a young brunette, Ayshem. She was the one who'd greeted and welcomed me. Last night, at the end of a day stitched together by violence and injustice, her kindness touched my very heart. As I was rambling on, unsteady from the shackles on my ankles, she showed me the around the premises, asleep at this hour: the rickety sink that let out a meagre trickle of icy water for 'washing up,' the plastic bucket for doing your business, the row of iron beds with their blankets that we were to squeeze into every night.

'Need any help washing up?' she asked. Gingerly, she rinsed out my hair. I stumbled from the weight of the chains, making her laugh. I was like one of those ridiculous clowns who pretend to get their feet caught up in a pair of pants too long for them. Once we'd shared this sudden burst of laughter, she made a spot for me among the sleeping women. 'How long have you been here?' I whispered as I bundled myself up in a synthetic blanket. 'Two months,' she replied.

Ayshem was 22 – almost the same age as Gulnigar. Her dark, silky hair fell all the way to her hips. She had been arrested because her mother-in-law had sent money to an acquaintance who'd sought asylum in Turkey. Probably one of her children, but Ayshem didn't want to say. When the police had come to their house, they'd taken everyone away: herself, her husband, her husband's mother. That was two months ago. Since then, she'd learned that her mother-in-law had lost the use of her legs while in detention. These days, they hauled her off to questioning in a wheelchair.

In the eyes of the authorities, Uyghurs who had lived abroad or knew people there posed the biggest threat. They were seen as spies. Judgment on the order of the 'Great Western Betrayal' lay in store for them. Ever since Ayshem was thrown in jail, the other women would say she'd been put away for 'political reasons.' We had that in common.

A voice crackled from the speaker affixed in the corner of the room. It spat out phrases in Mandarin that I couldn't understand. In Xinjiang, my Mandarin had been flawless, but at home we spoke Uyghur. I only used Mandarin at the company, when the situation demanded it. In France, I'd filed it away in a corner of my brain.

Huh – I hadn't noticed the cameras. In another corner, one of them was blinking. It turned to follow us when we crossed from sink to bed, bed back to sink. Bzzt, bzzt. It was unbearable. It mocked us, that camera. It humiliated us. I'd stare at it, trying to put all the wrath I had in my heart and soul into that stare. In my head I'd be pulverising it with my hateful looks, veiled by the tears that ran streaming down my cheeks. The crackling voice went on with its monologue. 'Number two? Present! Number three? Present!' When their numbers were called, the girls rose to their feet, standing stiff as boards at the edges of their beds. I followed suit, trembling.

This military ritual was one of several exercises. I never really knew if these were aimed at breaking down our minds, filling up our empty days, or 're-educating' us before we were even sent to the camps. At the time, I wasn't thinking much about that at all. I focused on the here and now of Cell 202: picking up codes of conduct to keep me from the dark thoughts that flooded my head the minute I had nothing to do. These rituals would also save me from the many punishments that the slightest misstep incurred. As soon as roll call was over, whispering resumed in the cell. In the ensuing murmur, Ayshem came over to me.

'Priority number one is learning those by heart,' she said, pointing at a rectangular poster on the main wall across from our straw mattresses. The rules for Cell 202 were listed there in Uyghur and Chinese. These were a series of mind-numbing duties and so-called rights that weren't really rights at all. We were to know them like the backs of our hands, because we had to recite them every morning. 'Often, the voice will pick one of us out at random. Then that person has to stand up with her arms straight by her sides and recite the rules in Mandarin,' my new friend explained. 'If you falter or can't remember, then you'll be punished.' Punished? What would they do to us? I stared at the rules on the cold grey wall. I took them in, not batting an eye. I didn't want to be punished. Ever. So I learned that:

- Speaking Uyghur is forbidden.
- Praying is forbidden.
- Fighting is forbidden.
- Hunger strikes are forbidden.
- If you are sick and require medical attention, refusing medical care is forbidden.
- Breaking the rules is forbidden.
- Drawing on the walls is forbidden.
- Poor hygiene is forbidden.

Among the rights, I made out the 'right to free worship' and the 'right to counsel.'

This was my first act of resistance. Learning everything by heart. Not giving them the chance or the pleasure of humiliating me with punishment.

5. Shackled to a Bed

I was punished, but I didn't know why. One morning the guard came in and, without a word, attached my chains to the bars of the bed. For two weeks, I'd been sitting on the dusty floor, my back against the metal bed. At night, I managed to pull myself up onto the mattress.

Around me, life in Cell 202 began over and over again beneath the relentless lighting that flattened all sense of night and day. So this was detention: a rotation of measly meals brought in by deaf-mute cooks chosen for their disability so they could not disclose what was afoot here. Congee or cornstarch slurry or cabbage soup. Stale bread. One egg a week. I lost a lot of weight – so much that my index fingers and thumbs met when I squeezed my waist. Detention was a parade of zombies adrift in orange jumpsuits, rings around their eyes. The room emptied and filled again like the old toilet we shared. In the daytime, the Chinese voice bawled through the speaker. It was in charge of our every movement, which the security camera always turned to follow. At night, that voice hounded me through the two or three hours of sleep I could manage.

When I'd arrived two and a half months ago, there were nine of us. Now there were almost 30, almost all Uyghur women. Their names escaped me. One of them had made the pilgrimage to Mecca, another was accused of selling banned religious CDs, others for having attended a wedding where no alcohol was served or the birthday party of a friend who wore a veil. Every day, Ayshem helped me wash up and do my business. She dried my hair with a square of sponge. Not long ago, she had taken to calling me 'Mama.'

The interrogations, imposed according to scheduling rules that escaped us, were the only thing that broke up the deadly monotony of our daily lives. They were my only hope. The guarantee that somewhere in a precinct in Xinjiang, officers were reviewing my file and weighing the accusations against me. The certainty that in France, Kerim, Gulhumar, and Gulnigar were moving heaven and earth to find out where I was. The more interrogation sessions I had, the less I would be forgotten.

In Cell 202, every summons to interrogation was an event. The voice from the intercom called on us by number. 'Number 7! Interrogation!' Number 7 would detach herself from the group and approach the door. We could already hear the bolts creaking. Heads would turn toward her, faces half-anxious, half-envious. Some people never came back from interrogation. They disappeared as abruptly as they had come, one winter night in the piercing fluorescence. No one ever knew what happened to them. Were they released? Some wished to believe so. I had no opinion myself. Each time my number was called, fear of a death sentence gripped my guts. But I doubted it. What I did know was that my case was giving them a hard time.

I was summoned to the interrogation room three times. 'That's a lot,' said the girls in my cell. 'It's a good sign,' Ayshem whispered. Kerim would've been proud of me. I never lost face in front of the policemen. I never broke down. That might've even been why they chained me to the bed. The last time, I'd gone too far.

It had been days ago. The way to the interrogation room led down a long, narrow, windowless passage with linoleum floors. The police cuffed my hands behind my back and pulled a smelly black woollen hood over my head. Through its weave, I could make out other cells along the hallway: 204, 206, 208.... They seemed empty, but I suspected they were full to bursting, just like Cell 202. Who were all these women crammed into each cell? To the left another hallway led off toward the interrogation rooms. A clicking of locks, heavy doors being pushed aside. An unseen hand pulled off my hood, leaving me face to face with Ablajan, one of the officers who'd been interrogating me from the start.

He was a Uyghur, a string bean of a man with a gaunt, pale face. He never wore a uniform. His smile might have seemed sympathetic had he not been my tormentor for two and a half months. Just like every other time, he ordered the guards to sit me down on the chair across from him. And just like every other time, the two guards escorting me unceremoniously obeyed. They clamped my throbbing wrists to two cuffs screwed into the chair arms, then left the room. A wall with a forest of bars atop it separated me from my interrogator. To his left lay a folder overflowing with photos and loose sheets of paper stamped at the bottom. My case file.

Every time, the wrestling match kicked off like this: Ablajan would open up the folder and flip through it nonchalantly, punctuating the silence of the room with little throat-clearing noises as if grimacing over this or that photo or document. It was like a gambler looking over his hand, weighing his strong suits and weaknesses. In the folder was the photo of Gulhumar waving the sky-blue flag of East Turkestan at the protest in Paris. Her laughing eyes and dazzling smile, stuck between a pay stub and a lease.

That photo is the backbone of that pile of papers, the only reason they're keeping me imprisoned in these four walls. Over the course of the interrogations, Ablajan has pulled it out several times and set it in plain sight on a corner of the table. For hours at a time, he punctuates his questions with the same sentence that brooks no appeal: 'Your daughter is a terrorist.' For hours at a time, I confront him with the same firm reply: 'No, my daughter is not a terrorist. I don't know why she was at that demonstration.'

To wear away at my already muddled mind, he set traps for me. The conversation turned to details of our lives as refugees in France: 'How is life in France? Good? What did you do for a job there?' Then he would suddenly slap a photo right under my nose, a photo of a Uyghur living abroad in exile.

'Ever seen this man before?'

'Never.'

'How about her? Or him?'

'I'm telling you, I have no idea who they are.'

These were lies. Sometimes the face of a friend or an acquaintance would pop up in the succession of photos taken during demonstrations in European capitals. But I never let on. If I gave Ablajan an opening, I was screwed: he'd report to his superior that I associated with terrorists. It'd be a one-way ticket to prison, or worse, a death sentence. So I gritted my teeth and rolled with the punches. I never let myself be caught off guard by his tactics. I knew them all, all the strings he'd tug at. The photos piled up before me. I was staggered by his collection of captured faces: women my age, men Kerim's age, but also younger faces, teenagers. What had we done wrong? All over the world, China was after Uyghur teens. What threat could an exiled teen possibly represent? The Communist Party was hunting us down like vermin.

The more I put up a fight, the more I realised that the thick folder full of charges was but a ploy to intimidate me. The conversation often dwelt on a host of administrative details from 2006, the time we'd left Xinjiang. Ablajan got lost in the bottomless well of Chinese paperwork that preceded any departure abroad: our apartment being put up for rent, our daughters being taken out of school, my unpaid leave from the company. His air of mistrust and his idiotic questions exasperated me. I was being held for 'stirring up unrest at a public assembly,' and this bureaucrat was nattering on about technical details?

'Why did France issue you a ten-year residency permit?'

'I don't know. That's standard procedure over there when you're a foreigner.'

'Your passport was only valid for five.'

'I renewed it at the embassy.'

'Does France give shelter to terrorists like you?'

'How should I know? Why don't you ask them?'

They obviously didn't have much on me. The proof? Threats and intimidation soon became the basis of those days spent with the red folder between us. At such times, as fatigue slowly crept up my spine, I thought of the bravery of Rebiya Kadeer, the face of Uyghurs living in exile abroad. From 1999 to 2005, she had been imprisoned in Ürümqi for 'state treason' for passing 'sensitive' documents on to her husband, a political refugee in the United States. Of her six years in prison, she spent two in solitary, confined to a two-metre (six-feet) square cell always sunken in darkness. She was a model of courage for the women of Cell 202. Thinking about her strength gave me strength of my own.

'We have spies in France. If you're lying, they'll tell us the truth. You should be afraid.'

'They'll be able to tell you I'm innocent! I'm not afraid, because I never did anything wrong!'

'If you keep this up, you'll never go back to France, do you hear me? You'll never see your husband and children again!'

'Well, I don't care. I don't care at all. As long as they're happy over there, I'm happy!'

I think I pissed him off that time.

❀ ❀ ❀

The shackles hurt. Ever since I'd been chained to the bed, my ankles hurt under their weight. Even if none of the windows gave any sign of it, the smell of spring was in the air of Cell 202. The adjoining door to our cell opened onto an enclosed but roofless courtyard with a square of sky above. Now and then, the guards would let us out to stretch our legs. The icy cold gnawing at the walls had recently given way to a light breeze, full of desert dust that dried out our eyes. For long minutes, we paced the beaten earth to the rhythm of orders from the loudspeaker. Chained to the bed as I was, I missed even this pitiful exercise.

I was like one of the walls of the room. I gazed mutely at the central square of space where the other girls were walking. Sometimes the guards would soften too, as if the milder weather eased their strictness. At five, before our nightly soup, some of us might be so bold as to start dancing. Uyghur music was forbidden here. No one even dared beg for it. So some of us imagined the notes to songs that were dear to us. They didn't hum out loud, but suddenly you could almost hear the notes echoing in the room while a few girls took a few timid steps. One of them would reach out a hand to her neighbour, and so on. Uyghur dance came back into its own in bodies that arched and spun as if to let skirts open up and whirl. During these brief respites, our faces with their features worn down by waiting relaxed. With a little imagination, I could see the sequins scintillating on vests, silk wrinkling between the legs of dancers as they leapt from one foot to another, the clatter of answering bracelets on wrists. Yes, with just a little imagination, I was reliving Gulhumar's wedding.

I liked watching the other women, but I've never liked dancing. Surprising, for a Uyghur. In Xinjiang, between the silence of the desert and the racket of mopeds, there is music with its *nagaras* (drums), *suonas* (oboes), and *dutars* (lutes). It shows up on street corners, at religious festivals, and receptions. Voices lament or exult over a bed of notes. I couldn't understand why they let us dance here, stuck between the dusty tile floor and the unflagging fluorescence. After robbing us of our dignity and our very name, why leave us this one last pleasure? Perhaps the better to take it away again a few minutes later. Perhaps also to allow us to believe that China's drive to wipe out Uyghur culture was only an illusion. That we'd made it all up.

And yet here we were, incarcerated. We who were guilty of nothing and yet guilty all the same. Such was the art of repression according to the Chinese Communist Party: banning everything while also allowing it. Reforming you while singing your praises. Imprisoning you while educating you. Not a single one of our friends in Karamay could assert with conviction that he'd been discriminated against since he was born. 'True, they've become mean,' whispered one friend at a dinner as I recounted my passport difficulties that January with embarrassment. Another said: 'It's getting harder and harder to find a job. Kerim was right.' But as always, discrimination dissolved in illusions of freedom: the folklore of music and dance that provincial administrators gave pride of place in official ceremonies, or compliments from Han people celebrating the beauty of Uyghur women.

When the music in our heads stopped with the guard's footfalls or static from the intercom announcing the soup hour, the women would stand there panting for a few more minutes, necks tense. Bodies interrupted, surprised in the intimacy of dance, wavered, still possessed by the imaginary notes as they faded away from Cell 202. Breathing slowed in phases, the dust settled once more into fine layer on the floor. Spirits returned to the dull and monotonous life of the cell. The women sat down cross-legged, sometimes in small circles. Night fell. Murmurs laden with memories of weddings and celebrations could be heard. A few laughs flowed into the wave of whispers.

We often talked about what it would be like afterwards, too. We inhabited an in-between space and time that might come to an end tomorrow or not for 100 days – who knew? Slumped across one another, eyes moist, some spoke of prison. They had brothers, uncles who'd already been locked away. Their voices grew choked as they piled on sordid, miserable details: torture, cold, rats, hunger, darkness. Each time, my heart would grow heavy as a stone, my stomach rumble with worry. I didn't want to go to prison. If I wound up there, I'd go under. I'd die.

Luckily, the girls also talked about 'schools': one step up from jail, sort of. After spending a decade in France, I was a novice when it came to repression. For the first time, I surmised the scope of the bunker that Xinjiang had become. I'd never heard of these mysterious educational establishments. The government had founded them to 'correct' Uyghurs, or so they said. And also, it was claimed, to help them find jobs. I didn't need a job. I lived in France. And even were I still in Karamay, I already had a job. I was a petroleum engineer! The women of Cell 202 also said that in these schools, you took courses taught by Han professors, just like in a regular school. Once their training was approved (it could take several months), students were free to return home.

I pictured classrooms full of wrinkled students with bags under their eyes, black hair shot through with white, wearing black and yellow uniforms like those Gulbahar and Gulnigar had donned every morning before going to the local school in Karamay. None of this filled me with confidence, but the state of my fatigue and fear had long since gotten the better of my reason. What could be worse than Cell 202? My fellow prisoners shared descriptions that made my mouth water: hot meals – a variety! – served up in a vast cafeteria from which students then retired to their dormitories in the early afternoon for a brief nap and again in the evening, for the night. In the bathroom, regimental rows of mirrors welcomed women's reflections; they were allowed to do their hair and put on makeup. And best of all, students could call their families. If I was ever sent to one of these schools, I could call Kerim or my sister Madina. I could tell them all about the nightmare from which I couldn't seem to wake up.

It was almost dinnertime. There was no clock around to confirm it, but my empty belly was in knots like a rag being wrung out to dry. While the girls argued over different versions of these schools, others began singing in low voices. 'My parents are waiting outside, I must go to them,' murmured several of them, curled up on the edge of the bed. It was a Uyghur poem. They sang it with their heads down so the tireless eye of the camera couldn't see their lips moving. Otherwise, they'd be accused of praying. They'd be confined to solitary in another cell, chained to the bed as I was at this moment. Others wept, listless and silent. A voice cut through the little group, loud and solemn: 'If your file's no good, they'll punish you. It's off to prison. If it's all right, they'll send you to school.'

I wanted to go to school. Good God, please make them send me to school.

6. Inside Cell 202

'Look! It's Gulbahar!'
    'Are you sure?'
'Yes. Yes! Look!'

The two policewomen guarding the entrance to the jail were standing in a sunbeam, excitedly chittering away like bush crickets as they snuck sidelong glances at me. Their shadows wriggled on the tiled lobby floor, a grey checkerboard streaked with dirt. Those tiles hadn't changed a bit. The months had carpeted them with dry powder brought in on the wind. The janitor kept this at bay with his broom, but little mounds of dirt presided here and there, in the corners of the vast lobby with its grimy roughcast walls. The last time my gaze had lingered on them was when I'd arrived in January. The policemen had waved a sheet of paper under my nose, a record of my confessions for 'stirring up public unrest.' A pen lay on the front counter, waiting for me to pick it up and sign the document. I was so paralysed by their yelling that I only made out terrifying snatches ('guilty,' 'terrorist,' 'spy'). I just kept staring at the grey grout lines between the tiles, my mind blank.

I was waiting in a dingy cell divided from the rest of the room by a forest of bars. It was where they put newcomers, but apparently also people on their way out, like me. In the middle of the cell stood a booth draped in black fabric, oddly reminiscent of a voting booth. When I'd first come in January, it had stunk of dirty socks as I'd slipped on my orange jumpsuit, shivering. I'd traded in my pile of clothes for filthy khaki leggings, a pair of stinking black slippers, a thin blanket, a plastic cup, and a toothbrush head: the sum of my personal affairs for the months to come.

In the same cell, which still stank of socks, I was now present for the same ritual in reverse. A stone-faced attendant brought me the clothes I'd been wearing that first day. Like me, they'd spent the winter locked up in a closet. In the darkness of the booth, I rid myself of my disgusting outfit, which I had trouble peeling off. The zipper on the jumpsuit was rusty; the rough cloth of its sleeves and legs was stiff from the cold, heat, and the sweat I'd been marinating in all these months. I'd never been issued with another one.

My detention had come to an end. Three days earlier, a police officer named Rahmanjan had summoned me. 'You're going to school,' was all he said. A wave of relief flooded my chest. When he saw my tense face relax into a tight smile, Rahmanjan gave me a wink. He told me my mother and sister had been by to drop off some things for me, but I wasn't allowed to see them. I gazed at him, uncomprehending, speechless, unable to keep the tears from flowing down my hollowed cheeks. Why tell me this now?

The news hung about me in a kind of fog. It was vital for me to get some perspective, focus on the here and now, which was full of hope: I was headed off to school! I wasn't going to rot away in some unhygienic prison for years. Instead, I'd be undergoing 'training'! If I showed proof of discipline and rigour in my work, I might even graduate 'in a few months.' Fine by me: I'd always been disciplined and rigorous.

The night before, the girls and I had done a lot of crying. Five of us in the cell had been chosen for school. My heart leapt when Ayshem told me she was one of them. Naturally, we all wondered what would happen to the others. Some burst into song while others braided my hair, buzzing around my head like flies. We laughed quietly. Now the end of the nightmare was at hand. All I had to do now was get dressed and deal with a few documents. Then I'd be out of here.

I was unsteady on my feet. My head spun. My entire naked body creaked like the tin roof on some old shack about to give way in a gust of wind. But I didn't feel like complaining. Happily I stuck one leg into my black pants, then the other. It felt so bizarre. They'd freed me from my shackles this morning, before I left Cell 202. When the tiny key broke off in the rusted keyhole, they had to resort to furious hammering. My ankles still bore scars: rust deposits printed on my skin like the designs brides-to-be paint in henna on their bodies.

The skin on my back, which had once bulged over my bra strap here and there, now lay smooth beneath the pressure from the elastic. My breasts recovered their swell in the cups of black lace. After all this time, a trace of my perfume remained: Narciso Rodriguez. I rediscovered the refined blend of musk and rose with a faint afternote of patchouli. Time had been at work on this bra as it lay buried in a locker. Back in Boulogne, I used to spritz my upper chest twice with the scent every morning. The vial of perfume was likely tucked away in a corner of my suitcase, abandoned in a guest room at my mother's in Ghulja. Poor Mama... she must've been worried sick.

Soon I was back in my black trousers. A thin, faded sweater clung to a waist now stripped of its former curves. I reacquainted myself with this body, circumspect but not saddened. For lack of a mirror, I explored it with the palms of my hands, attentive to the battlefields left by malnutrition, fear, and insomnia. It was as if I'd been given a new housing of flesh. In the dimness of the booth, I was taking ownership of it. Weirdly enough, I found a certain allure to the thinness of my wrists and ankles, the curve of my bottom and the tautness of my navel. Wasn't a traumatised, worn-out prisoner supposed to feel disgust or even hatred for her own body? After all, it was the reflection of her ordeal. With every exhausted breath she let out, every time she glimpsed her newly bony self in the mirror, it would remind her. But that wasn't the case with me. On the contrary, the vanity of being reunited with my clothes filled me with strength. It was frivolous, but I think I even felt beautiful.

In my family, the Haitiwajis, we've always had a certain respect for our appearance, and this has been passed down from one generation to the next. It's not that we worship beauty, which is entirely subjective, but rather that we are sharp dressers: the women take care to bedeck themselves with jewels, ribbons, fabrics, and fragrances. Femininity passes from mother to daughter, much like hospitality and generosity. It resides in the discerning choice of clothes, but also in the setting of a table and the spicing of a sauce. I can still recall Gulhumar crying as a little girl when I'd button her up in a white satin robe. She'd stamp her feet in the bathroom, exasperated by these outfits ill-suited to biking around the alleyways of Karamay. In return, I'd whip up a storm when she came home all dishevelled and hurry her into the hot shower, from which she emerged red as a crab. It wasn't easy for her – she'd much rather have been a boy – or for me, heir to a cumbersome legacy of femininity. I tried to mould her and, sulky and quick-tempered, she refused the mould. Too constricting. Too uncomfortable. Deep down, I admired her courage.

The wheeze of an engine shutting off brought me back to the booth in the cell. Through the curtain, I could make out a few policemen moving about the lobby. Only one final item of clothing remained: a soft turtleneck, too warm for the summery climate. I put it on, taking care not to undo the braids in my hair, and then left the foul-smelling booth behind. The bolt turned in the metal door. I was outside.

Wallet. Identity card. Residency permit. Money. None of these. At the station's front desk, I didn't get any of the things people usually get back when they are released from custody. What had happened to the purse I was carrying the day I was arrested in January? What had the police done with it? Had they destroyed it? The thought that my residency permit had been incinerated or torn into tiny pieces made my heart sink. How would I ever get back to France if my residency permit was gone? But my anguish was already dissipating. I could hear whispers interspersed with chuckles from the two policewomen at the entrance.

'Ooh, she's gotten herself all dolled up!'

'She's lost some weight! I hardly recognise her!'

Exhilarated by the brightness outside and the tune of their flattery, I brushed by them with what I hoped was a steady, assured step. They smiled as I passed, as if we were old friends. 'Goodbye, Gulbahar,' one of them said. I barely spoke a word. The down jacket I'd been wearing in January was under one arm. It gave me composure as I left that hell without looking back. No way was I letting them think that the congee, the chains, and the blinding fluorescence of Cell 202 had broken me. With my hands full, I rediscovered the delicious feeling of freedom that comes with the act of moving toward a goal: the car with the tinted windows that awaited me, one door open, in the parking lot next to the jail. Several women were already there and waiting. Eyes half-shut, I savoured the traces of patchouli that still wafted from my brassiere. For a fleeting moment, the scent tickled my nostrils, just long enough for me to rush down the three steps at the entrance and cross the courtyard of beaten earth where a few policemen were puffing on cigarettes while scratching at the ground with the tips of their shoes. I didn't know what lay in store, but anything had to be better than Cell 202. The door slammed shut behind me. A powerful blast of air conditioning dispelled Narciso Rodriguez. Next stop: 'school.'

7. 'School' with Xi Jinping

10th June 2017

'Right! Left! At ease!' There were 40 of us in the room, all women, wearing blue pyjamas. It was a nondescript rectangular classroom, no more than 50m² (500 square feet). A big metal shutter, perforated with tiny holes that let the light in, hid the outside world from us. Eleven hours a day, the world was reduced to this room. Our slippers squeaked on linoleum as two Han soldiers relentlessly kept time. This was called 'physical education.' In reality, it was tantamount to military training. Our exhausted bodies moved through the space in unison, back and forth, side to side, corner to corner. When the soldier bellowed 'At ease!' in Mandarin, our regiment of prisoners froze. He would then order us to remain still. This could last half an hour, or just as often a whole hour, or even several. When it did, our legs would begin to prickle all over with pins and needles. Our bodies, still warm and restless, struggled not to sway in the moist heat. We could smell our own foul breath. We panted like oxen. Sometimes, one or another of us would faint. If she failed to come to on her own, a guard would yank her to her feet and slap her awake. If she collapsed again, he would drag her out of the room, and we'd never see her again. Ever. At first, I found this shocking. Before long, it was just business as usual.

I'd been here for three days now. When I wasn't on the verge of tears, I sometimes stifled a giggle over what a ridiculous spectacle it was: the two men in their martial tones choreographing us, 40 little ersatz soldiers. We stood in impeccable ranks facing a portrait of Xi Jinping, moon face and paternalistic smile against an azure blue background. You'd think we were in Tiananmen Square. Stuck in his frame, he watched us march back and forth across the room, hands obediently folded behind our backs, like in the annual military parades. I wanted to scream in his face that I'd remain a free woman for the rest of my life, that his system would never break me.

Three days I'd been here. They'd told us training would last for two weeks. After that, the theory classes would begin. I didn't know how I was going to hold out. How had I not broken down already? This was Baijiantan. That was all the information I'd managed to glean after leaving the jail, from a sign stuck in a dried-out ditch where a few empty plastic bags drifted about. Baijiantan was on the outskirts of Karamay, a no-man's-land from which three buildings rose, each the size of a small airport. Beyond the barbed-wire fence, there was nothing but desert as far as the eye could see.

Among the 40 new arrivals were petite older women stooping in the thick cloth of their blue pyjamas, wilting teens lost in the billows of the same, and women like me, hunched over from exhaustion and sleepless nights on a straw mattress. Nadira was one of these, too. There she stood, perfectly erect in the row of women facing me. She was the only person I really made a connection with. I met her the first day. When the female guards opened the door to my 'room,' she was waiting there alone, in the middle of the dormitory with its row of numbered wooden planks: our beds. Nadira was in Bunk No. 8. I was assigned Bunk No. 9. That coincidence was enough to draw us together. My arrival had made her feel better; she'd been there for several hours. One of the first things she asked was: 'Why do you smell so good?' I told her about the bra I'd recovered from the locker at the jail. We had a good laugh. Her sparkling eyes inspired confidence. For once, I wasn't suspicious. 'We can share it, if you want,' I said. 'The bra, I mean. I'll just set it between our beds at night, and that way we can both smell it.' She liked that idea. 'Oh, you'd do that? That's so nice, Gulbahar! Thank you!'

In exchange for the wafts of Narciso Rodriguez, she showed me around the dormitory, which still reeked dizzyingly of fresh paint: the bucket for doing your business, which she gave a wrathful kick; the window with its metal shutter always drawn tight; the two cameras panning back and forth in high corners of the room. That was it. No real mattress to speak of. No furniture. No toilet paper. No sheets. No sink. Just two of us in the gloom and the muffled bang of heavy cell doors slamming shut.

That first day, Nadira did a lot of talking. She paced around the room like a caged tiger, hurling scraps of her story at the walls. She had been a TV host on a cultural channel in Karamay. A 'terrific show' broadcast in the Uyghur language, a 'nice way to spend the evening,' she added as I looked on, flabbergasted. She'd wanted to become a professional dancer, do opening ceremonies for political officials in Xinjiang. That hadn't panned out, but TV was a respectable consolation prize. You were still on a stage with the spotlights, the energy of a live audience. Besides, Nadira had a special look to her – the kind of beauty that the 'lights took a shine to,' as she put it. It was her thing. She lived with her husband and children in a pretty house downtown. One day, plainclothes agents had showed up at her door. 'Did you know that prayer is forbidden?' they asked. 'I don't know how they found out. Sure, I prayed every now and then,' she whispered as if the cameras could hear us (and maybe they could). They hadn't said where they were taking her. All she'd heard was the same word I had: 'school.' Next thing she knew, she'd found herself in Baijiantan. I realised that this was no school. It was a 're-education' camp.

❀ ❀ ❀

We were also taught patriotic songs while standing in formation. 'You must learn them by heart, or you will be punished.' All day long, we croaked out these refrains. Since Nadira had a pretty voice, the two soldiers had given her a special task. At their command, she would step forward from the ranks and go stand beside them. Lifting her right hand, she would launch into the national anthem and, on her signal, the rest of our voices, husky from being silenced too often, rose in the classroom: 'Stand up! Stand up! Stand up! We are billions of one heart, braving the enemies' fire. March on! Braving the enemies' fire, march on! March on! March on! On!' It was ridiculous.

In Cell 202, we had been left to our own devices. Idleness, our daily burden, stripped away our ability to think. Tedium alone, across drawn-out stretches of time, occupied our minds. For whole days at a time, we were dying of boredom. Oh my God, we were bored! Round and round in circles we'd go when all we wanted was to leave, run away, scream.

Here, the military rules were designed to break us. Sheer physical fatigue robbed us of the desire to speak. Our days were punctuated by the screech of whistles: on waking, at mealtime, at bedtime. Lunches and dinners followed one after another, during which we were not allowed to speak. The guards always had an eye on us. If one of us whispered or wiped her mouth, she was accused of praying. If one of us turned down her food, she was called an 'Islamist terrorist' and ordered to polish off her plate. The wardens claimed our food was halal. We had no choice but to eat it. At night, I would collapse on my bunk in a stupor. I had lost all sense of time. There was no clock. I guessed at the hour of day from how cold or hot it felt. I lived in terror of the guards.

We hadn't seen daylight since we arrived. All the windows were blocked by those metal shutters. Left to my own devices, I debated with myself. But what was the point of wasting what little energy I had left? We were surrounded by desert as far as the eye could see. Rahmanjan had promised I'd be given a phone, but none had materialised. Apart from him, who else even knew I was being held here? Had my sister been notified, or Aynur? Kerim and Gulhumar? It was a waking nightmare. I couldn't even open up to my fellow detainees because the cameras were always watching. I was tired, so tired. I couldn't even think anymore.

Naptime was my salvation. After lunch, the guards would lead us back to our cells, where we were allowed to lie down on our straw mattresses for about half an hour. Some of my fellow detainees took the chance to doze off; others stayed awake and whispered. For me, that time was a retreat into my secret garden. No one could keep me from going there. It was inside my head. Every day, to the soothing sound of Nadira's regular breathing, I cultivated happy memories. They reminded me where I was from. Thanks to them, I managed not to be completely overwhelmed. Half-asleep, I picked up the train of my thoughts where I'd left off the night before. Barcelona, Fontainebleau, the gardens at Giverny, the little towns in the Yvelines we'd drive through on Sundays, the trunk of our car full of fruits, vegetables, and flowers from La Ferme de Viltain. I cared for these memories lovingly in order of preference, sorting them chronologically, bringing them back to life with countless details. 'What are you thinking about?' Nadira would often murmur, her voice thick. Tears would spring to my eyes. My throat tightened. I didn't want to start crying in front of the camera. Instead, I stared at the white ceiling. 'Nothing,' I said. 'Nothing.'

Baijiantan is a massive labyrinth. A handful of guards would escort us to each of our activities in groups, by dormitory. Once naptime was over, even a moment's privacy was impossible.

To reach the bathrooms, classrooms, or mess hall required navigating a series of endless fluorescent-lit hallways. At their far ends, automatic security doors sealed off the maze like airlocks. One thing was for sure: all this had just sprung up from the ground. Everything here was new. The reek of paint from the spotless walls was a ubiquitous reminder of that fact.

It seemed like the premises of a factory, but I didn't yet have a handle on just how big it was. In Baijiantan, daily life came down to a triangular ambit: cell – classroom – mess hall. Only the sheer number of prisoners and guards whose paths we crossed when being herded around in a group gave me an inkling of just how enormous the camp really was. Every day, I saw new faces, zombie-like, bags under the eyes. So far, I had never seen the same group of prisoners twice. The first day, Nadira and I had been the only ones in our cell. By that night, there were seven of us. Now there were twelve.

A little quick maths: I'd counted 16 cells, including mine, each with twelve bunks, twelve prisoners crammed in on top of each other. Multiply the number of cells by the number of prisoners, and that made for almost 200 detainees at Baijiantan. Two hundred women torn from their families. Two hundred lives locked up until further notice. And the camp just kept getting ever fuller before our very eyes.

You could tell the new arrivals from their distraught faces. They still tried to meet your gaze in the hallway. The ones who'd been there for longer looked down at their feet. They shuffled around in close ranks, like robots. They snapped to attention without batting an eye, whenever a whistle ordered them to. Good God, what had been done to make them that way? I shuddered at the thought of finding out.

Shortly after my arrival, something unusual happened. I ran into a woman I knew. It happened in the bathroom, a huge tiled space with aluminium sinks lining one wall but not a single mirror. There were only seven showers and five toilets, all Turkish. I was scouring my face with icy water at one of the sinks. In the morning, every second counted. We were only given 15 minutes to do a quick wash-up, go to the bathroom, and put on our blue jumpsuits. If we didn't finish fast enough, the guards would force us out of the room anyway. That was the only time all day we were allowed to relieve ourselves. I wasn't about to miss my turn. I never had any notion of the time, but I was always trying to gauge how many minutes I had left. So that morning, when I heard my name, I wasn't exactly paying attention to the voice at first. 'Gulbahar?' I turned around, dripping, annoyed at being bothered during my daily sprint. I didn't recognise her right away, what with the weight she'd lost and her newly grey hair. 'Dilnur!' I wanted to give her a hug. But we weren't allowed to touch each other. We maintained a few inches between us as we stood in the middle of the tiled room.

She was crying. 'How did you wind up here? Didn't you go to France? Did they take your husband too? Mine's been in a camp for weeks, just like me.' Dilnur had been our neighbour in Karamay. Our interactions had been limited to thank-yous over small favours, but we'd been friendly. She loved our daughters a great deal and would watch over them when I worked late. I remembered her as a sweet, gentle woman. Now she was a shadow of herself. They'd broken her. Between sniffles, she told me her story. They'd turned up one morning and arrested her husband for no reason, probably because he regularly went to mosque. They'd thrown him in a camp not far from Baijiantan; she didn't know which one. Then, without bringing up any real charges against her, they'd sent her here for an unspecified length of time. How could they have put her, of all people, in a camp? I knew her. She and her husband were moderate Muslims. She didn't wear a veil, nor did she espouse separatist beliefs. She was an ordinary woman, just another Uyghur from Karamay, one of thousands. Were they going to arrest every Uyghur in the city?

8. Nadira Vanishes

20th June 2017

They took Nadira. They vanished her. One morning, she was summoned along with two other women. We were still doing our forced march in the classroom. Our legs felt heavy. It was stiflingly hot that day, and although we'd asked to have the iron shutters opened up to let the air in, the policemen wouldn't hear of it. 'At ease!' As usual, we froze, and then... Rahmanjan burst into the room, accompanied by two other officers. 'Number 8!' he shouted. Nadira stepped meekly forward. The two other women, both younger than I was, did the same when they heard their numbers. I could feel my legs shaking. Nothing good would come of this. I hadn't seen Rahmanjan since I left the jail. If he was here for her, something serious must have happened. All this took less than half a second. I craned my neck for a glimpse of what was happening up at the head of the line. Without a word, the officers cuffed the three women. Then they were gone. We never saw them again. Before falling in behind the group, Rahmanjan turned toward us: 'These women are being taken away because they have not confessed to their crimes. Confess, or else it will soon be your turn.' The door closed behind them. The forced march resumed.

During naptime, the incident was all we talked about. Where had they been taken? But most of all, why? Some who knew them well claimed they'd been sent to prison because of their relations with a Muslim priestess in Karamay. I'd heard of her before, back when we used to live here. Her name was Rizwan Bawudun, and she gave workshops and lectures on Islam. She would popularise passages from the Qur'an for small gatherings. Often, the most devout families would ask her to give speeches at weddings or funerals. She performed purification rituals. Nadira had never told me she and her were close.

Her straw mattress, next to mine, remained empty for two days, and then a new woman replaced her. I eyed her with mistrust as she moved in. That was when it really hit me: Nadira wasn't coming back. She was probably rotting away in a dark cell in Karamay. I hoped they hadn't sentenced her to death.

At night, we'd wake with a start to terrifying screams, as if someone was being tortured upstairs. We listened in silence, absolutely still, to howls that pierced the night. They were the cries of women going mad, begging guards not to hurt them anymore. They also asked forgiveness for their crimes.

They'd made an example of Nadira. Ever since she'd left our cell, the guards had had a field day with us. They were more vicious than ever. On top of the military drills, we now had to face swarms of insults. These came raining down on us at the slightest misstep: 'Filthy terrorist.' 'Why don't you eat pork, eh?' All day long, the guards would keep telling us that we were guilty of the 'most heinous crime,' that of 'betraying our great homeland.' They called us the 'criminals' from the 2009 Ürümqi riots: 'Confess your crimes! Or else you'll end up in prison like Nadira and all the rest! Write out your self-criticism, and the Party may forgive you!'

I'd thought the theory classes would bring us some relief, but they were even worse. The teacher was always watching us. She slapped us every chance she got. One day, one of my classmates, a woman in her sixties, shut her eyes, from exhaustion or fear. The proctor gave her a brutal slap. 'Think I don't see you praying? You'll be punished!' The guards dragged her violently from the room. An hour later, she came back with something she'd written: her self-criticism. The teacher made her read it out to us. She obeyed, ashen-faced, then sat down. All she'd done was shut her eyes. What were we even guilty of? All around me, I saw nothing but trembling old women and teenage girls on the brink of tears. We weren't terrorists.

The classroom, the bathroom, the mess hall, the cell: there was nowhere in Baijiantan where we were not subject to violence or coercion from the teachers, police officers, and guards. Even when they weren't on our backs, the cameras were still watching us. We were reduced to living like disposable creatures, eternal victims bowed under the weight of threats.

Instead of getting me down, Nadira's disappearance hit me like an electric shock. I'd become tougher since the days when being chained to my bed in Cell 202 had reduced me to tears. They wouldn't see me cry. Their attempts to break me would come to nothing. I made a promise to myself as I fell asleep that night, the first without Nadira by my side. In my secret garden, where I kept my memories, I dug up a little square of dirt. There I planted the seeds of my resistance. I would survive the hell that was Baijiantan.

I had never been a devout believer, but now I turned to God. In defiance, perhaps. At night, my eyes shut, I prayed with all my strength. In my cell, morning and evening, I forced myself to do yoga. No way was I about to let them turn me into a shapeless wreck, I stood up in the middle of my cell, facing the camera. I breathed in, widened my stance, hands on my hips. I breathed out, folding my chest towards my legs. As the blood drained slowly to my head, I prayed. There was no way for the camera to spot my murmuring to God. Hands together between my breasts, upper body pressed to my legs, I begged for someone to come and rescue me, for my family to be safe. How good it felt to fool the cameras and their unblinking gaze.

These little acts of resistance multiplied my strength. Since classes had begun, I'd needed it even more. I'd been full of illusions when the military training had ended, one week after Nadria disappeared. I did my utmost to play the diligent schoolgirl and model prisoner. Rahmanjan's words came to me: if I excelled at my classes, I'd get out of Baijiantan sooner. My efforts would be rewarded.

But this wasn't the school I'd hoped for. After a few days, I understood what people meant by 'brainwashing.'

In truth, this was no school at wall. There were no bells to signal the end of class. There were no right or wrong answers. Every morning, a Uyghur instructor would come into our silent classroom. A woman of our own ethnicity, teaching us how to be Chinese. She treated us like wayward citizens that the Party had to 'reeducate.' I wondered what she thought of all this. Did she think anything at all? Where was she from? How had she ended up here? Had she herself been 're-educated' before taking on this work? My head was buzzing with questions.

At her signal, we all stood up as one. *Lao shi hao*! This greeting to the teacher kicked off eleven hours of daily 'education.' We recited a kind of pledge of allegiance to China: 'Thank you to our great country. Thank you to our Party. Thank you to our dear President Xi Jinping.' In the evening, a similar version ended the lesson: 'I wish for my great country to develop and have a bright future. I wish for all ethnicities to form a single great nation. I wish good health to President Xi Jinping. Long live President Xi Jinping.' Glued to our chairs, we echoed these words like parrots. We were instructed in China's glorious history, washed clean of all its abuses. The cover of our textbooks read: 'Re-education Programme.' It told only of distinguished dynasties, glorious conquests, and the triumph of the Communist Party in its every undertaking. It was even more biased and politicised than what is taught at Chinese universities. At first, it made me laugh. Did they really think they could break us with a few pages of propaganda?

But the days went by, and with nothing in the offing but school, fatigue set in like an old enemy. I was exhausted, and my firm resolve to resist was put on permanent hold. I tried not to give in, returning to my garden every day, but the steamroller of school went on. It rolled right over our aching bodies. So this was brainwashing, whole days spent repeating the same idiotic phrases. As if that weren't enough, we had to do an hour of extra study after dinner in the evening, before going to bed. We would review our endlessly repeated lessons one last time. Every Friday, we had an oral and a written test. One by one, as a handful of the camp's superintendents looked warily on, we would regurgitate the Communist stew we'd been served up.

One lesson followed another. No sooner had we taken something in than we had to spit it back out. As a result, I never remembered anything from one week to the next. I was incapable of reciting what I'd learned just six days ago. I'd try to grab at snatches here and there, but the words all just bounced around in my head. The ideas sank away in a fog. They slipped between my fingers like water and, defeated, I watched them go.

When conscripted in this way, our short-term memory became our best friend and worst enemy. It allowed us to assimilate and recall countless chapters of history and citizens' declarations, thus sparing us the public humiliation the teacher would hand out. But at the same time, it wore away our critical faculties. It distanced us from the memories and thoughts that kept us alive.

The faces of Kerim, Gulhumar, and Gulnigar grew blurry. We were no longer anything but animals dumbed down by labour. The entirety of our lives was devoted to study for an undetermined amount of time. No one told us how long all of this would go on. We had no other prospects in the days or even the months ahead. When I thought about it, I felt sick to my stomach. Burying myself in work was much easier.

9. A Reunion with Hope

14th July 2017

Since my arrival in Baijiantan, I could think of only one thing: seeing my mother and my two sisters, Nedjma and Madina, again. I am the fifth of eight children. As in most big families where siblings are staggered across several generations with bigger or smaller gaps between, growing up farther or closer apart, I felt closest to my two younger sisters. I saw my older brothers on the major holidays of Eid and Nowruz, but right from the start, my younger sisters and I were inseparable, as my mother had raised the three of us together. Nedjma was the next youngest. These days, she is a housewife who spends most of her time taking care of our mother, widowed over 20 years ago, as well as seeing to my mother's house, her errands and paperwork. Nedjma and her own family live under my mother's roof, in the same house in Ghulja where all eight of us grew up. I have never known a kinder person.

Then there is Madina. Madina and her bursts of booming laughter. Madina and the funny faces she pulled, always ready to make you guffaw at the dinner table. Madina and her boundless generosity. She lives in the capital city of Ürümqi with her husband and their two children. I love both of my younger sisters very much, but Madina, the youngest, is the one I feel closest to. Maybe it's because we followed the same path upon finishing college, moving to bustling cities far from our brothers and sisters, from our mother's house, from Ghulja and its mountains. I discovered Karamay and its oil, while she found Ürümqi and its economic boom. No doubt another thing we had in common emerged over the years: we were women with jobs at a time when, like Nedjma, most women limited themselves to motherhood and domestic life.

Anxiously, I pressed the guards. 'When will I see my family? Have you told them I'm here? I was told I could see them! Let me see them – please, I'm begging you!' All they ever said was, 'Not right away. We'll see, we'll see.' The guards at Baijiantan replied to our questions in ways that were vague enough to keep us hoping and yet sink our spirits at the same time: 'Be patient.' 'Not just yet.' When our requests didn't get us a categorical 'No!' or a slap for 'insolence,' they were left hanging. The same rule applied for any kind of entreaty: going to the bathroom in the middle of the night, getting a visitor or a telephone call. Some nights, I could hear the women in other cells begging guards to be allowed to go to the bathroom. They were weeping, screaming, banging on the walls. Sometimes, a guard would give in, and I'd hear the litany of bolts being turned in locks, and then footsteps on the linoleum of the hallway that led to the bathroom. But other times, the guards made no reply, and our only choice was to urinate in the cell.

Weeks passed. All notion of time disappeared. Until today. Today I received an unexpected visit. At last. I'd stopped believing it would ever come to pass. But nothing about the visit went like I'd thought it would. Something awful happened.

When the security gate opened, revealing them, my heart leapt in my chest. After months alone, without a single familiar face, I now saw them coming toward me in the visiting room: my mother's slender frame, her long dress out of place in the sickly ambiance where a few detainees whispered with their loved ones, bodies hunched over tiny tables, hands sometimes joined. My mother's features were hardened by fatigue, or maybe by something I couldn't put my finger on that told me, before she even opened her mouth, she was the bearer of bad tidings. Nedjma followed closely behind. She, too, seemed to be distracted, her thoughts elsewhere. Only when the doors closed behind them and Madina's joyous face hadn't appeared did I realise something serious had befallen my youngest sister.

I knew Madina and Nedjma had moved heaven and earth in an attempt to free me, using their connections in the capital and even trying to bribe police officers. Madina would never have willingly missed this moment. So when my mother and Nedjma told me that Madina hadn't been able to find anyone to look after her children so she could make the trip, I did not believe them. She had been prevented from coming. I was sure of it.

The conversation moved onto a succession of banal details, the little things that make up everyday life but which seemed all the more frivolous to me since one of the usual participants was missing. We chatted as if we were sipping tea, carefully sidestepping the ongoing nightmare of the last seven months. No one asked about the jail in Karamay or the living conditions here. Not another word about Madina. I didn't bring up the deleterious instruction here at school, or the sleepless nights. We didn't even comment on the visiting area, full of women in convict jumpsuits. Their prattle rang in my ear, a distant echo. My mother's fragile health, cousins up north, Nedjma's children, her husband. I scrutinised their exhausted faces, and they mine. We were barely listening to each other, for only one question hovered, unanswered, over the heavy silences that punctuated our discussion, which we wanted to seem as natural as possible to the guards: where was Madina?

Nedjma cracked first. 'They took her too,' she let slip in a barely audible whisper, smothered by the echo of conversations around us. 'They'? They who? The police? Where did they take her? Jail, like me? My heart was pounding so hard in my chest that I could feel its each and every beat. I kept sneaking glances from the corner of my eye at the warder strolling through the room. Then I understood. Madina was in a camp. A camp like this one, in Baijiantan. A vast windowless warehouse reeking of fresh paint, sweat, and death, built from scratch just a few months ago, to which the regime's good little soldiers were shuffling women off by the hundreds. Madina was one of them. Tears welled up, filling my eyes, blurring my vision. I blinked them away, my throat tight, recalling the warder who'd warned me loudly as I came in: 'No crying, got it? Cry, and your visiting rights are over. These'll be the last visitors you ever get!' My God, they'd taken Madina.

Nearby, the security gates kept opening to admit unfamiliar faces: mothers, sisters, daughters made their way among the tables. I watched as they sat down across from the detainees, as my mother and Nedjma had done just a few minutes earlier. My sister's clipped explanations were making my head spin. They'd jailed Madina over some murky administrative affair. Something to do with an invalid certificate of residence. Expired papers. I wasn't really following.

In China, you can't just live wherever you want. To move to a place where you've found a job, you must first obtain a *hukou*. This precious regional passport allows you to settle in a city of your choosing, and it seemed the police in Ürümqi were claiming Madina's *hukou* was not in order, although she'd lived in Ürümqi for years. What would they do to her?

The minutes flew by. Time always went faster in the visiting area, and once again, I was tracking the warder's every move for fear he'd suddenly end this visit. I burned with the desire to ask them if they'd tried calling Boulogne. I was imagining Kerim's voice at the other end of the line, suddenly breaking off when he heard Nedjma's squawking. Then it was my turn to crack. My questions came down like hail, all at once: 'How are they? How's Kerim? And Gulhumar? And Gulnigar?' My mother said nothing. Nedjma took my hands. 'Everyone's fine, really. Don't worry. The one thing you mustn't do is worry,' she insisted. The small talk resumed. 'How's the food here? Have you met other women?' The more tightly her hands gripped mine, the less I wanted to tell her about women screaming at night, or how we got slapped around without warning. Madina must've been hearing those same screams, getting those same slaps. My heart was beating fit to burst. Suddenly, I felt a hurry to wrap things up. I glanced at the guard posted a yard away from our table. 'I get enough to eat. They treat us well here. Don't worry. Tell them I'm doing fine, will you?'

The visit from Nedjma and my mother confirmed something for me: if one person from a Uyghur family gets detained, they will drag all the others down with them. Madina hadn't been sent to a camp over some red tape. If Madina had really been having problems with her *hukou*, she wouldn't be in a camp, she'd be at home with her husband and children. They'd locked her up because of me. It was my fault, and I'd have to live with that guilt forever. Me, her 'terrorist' sister who'd lived abroad, married to a political asylee. Without meaning to, I'd brought the wrath of the authorities down on her head. Maybe they were torturing her to make her confess to 'crimes' that I refused to confess to. I refused because I hadn't done anything. She hadn't done anything either. We were both innocent.

No one in Xinjiang is free to say what they think. Nedjma and my mother might not have been rotting away in a camp, but they, too, were serving time. Their mouths were gagged, just like mine. Beyond the forest of barbed wire around Baijiantan, the 're-education' of Uyghurs was proceeding apace. Whether they locked us up or not, China reserved one fate and one fate alone for us all: 're-education' through fear, coercion, and censorship. Without distinction, they ground us all underfoot in the open-air prison that Xinjiang had become.

Imagine the fear they lived in, my poor mother, my poor sister Nedjma. Police dropping by unannounced, invitations to the police station for 'tea,' relentless interrogations.... I know they hadn't told me everything, but how could I blame them? Long before the camps appeared, we were already lying by omission, the better to protect one another. We never told each other everything.

When it came time to say goodbye and we were sharing a quick hug, I couldn't help myself. I might never get another chance like this anytime soon, and I had to know. 'Is Kerim in Xinjiang?' I whispered in Nedjma's ear. 'No, no, he's not here,' she whispered back.

'Do you swear? Tell him not to come, it's too dangerous. I know he probably wants to come free me, but if he comes, they'll take him too! Tell him not to do it. Please. Our daughters are the most important thing.'

Nedjma promised to tell him. 'And Madina?' I added as the guard approached.

'Don't worry. We're doing everything we can to get her out. Another two weeks, I think,' she said.

We smiled at each other, and then I watched as the automatic doors closed on their retreating figures. They were back in their prison, and I in mine.

10. 'Re-education' is Working

3rd September 2017

Like a Chinese school – an actual one where children learn Mandarin, literature, maths, history, and geography – Baijiantan, a fake school but a very real internment camp, had begun adorning itself in the red and gold of Communism: lanterns, banners, and the other paper decorations that Han teachers and children hang everywhere before celebrating the national holiday. In August, China honoured the People's Liberation Army and, although cut off from the world for months, we prisoners would not be spared an occasion to pay tribute to the Communist Party. The Party in its munificence had given us a chance to redeem our 'sins' through 're-education.' We owed it at least that much.

Patriotic songs, especially the national anthem, were so deeply ingrained in my mind that I could no longer forget them. Lying on my straw mattress at night, my body still tense from the day's stresses, I would fall into a restless sleep filled with proctors, uniformed men, fellow detainees, and Chinese flags. I could even hear one of my cellmates humming one of the choruses drummed into our heads that day.

Baijiantan also borrowed a spirit of competition from Chinese schools. The women of every cell had to sing before the camp's superintendents, who evaluated their performance. The winning cell took home a prize – probably food, or maybe new clothes. Without realising it, the competitive spirit that reigned in the days before the holiday insinuated itself into our minds, such that even after lessons were over we found ourselves rehearsing patriotic songs at night, in our cells. Little by little, this tactic for recreational 're-education' got the better of my vigilance. When I still had the presence of mind to do so, I told myself time and again that all this was but a tissue of lies I was pretending to believe while preserving my capacity to think critically. Stupidly, I let myself be caught up in the game. Once the bolts slid into place behind us, the day's exercises resumed at prompting from one of us. 'Should we practise?' someone would say. A shiver of excitement would run through the group. So practise we did. Lined up impeccably along our bunks, facing an audience of invisible superintendents, we all straightened our arms alongside our bodies and, like the other women in neighbouring cells, launched into the national anthem as one. 'Re-education' was working.

I indulged in this ridiculous game because a Big Day was coming. I nourished in my heart of hearts an immense happiness, bigger than anything else. It gave me the sudden feeling that my body was indestructible. The police might manage to make me caterwaul every patriotic song in the land, sleep with the lights on for years at a time, or stuff my head with Xi Jinping's political triumphs, but never again could they do me any harm. On 13th August, the Ürümqi police had freed Madina from her ordeal. As soon as she was released, my dearest little sister had rushed to find me in Baijiantan, and this flash of life, fleeting but incredibly intense, had given me enough joy to confront every misfortune the world had to offer.

When the Big Day came, Madina showed up laden with presents: arms carrying crates of donut peaches with their downy white skin, candies and sheep's milk cheese in her bag. She had spent 39 days in a camp and knew that detainees were never given such rare foodstuffs. But she also knew that the police, themselves weary of the vile food served here, would be greedily eyeing the gifts. Maybe they'd buy her a few extra minutes of visiting time or, better yet, make them kinder toward me. Madina was proven right. I'd barely laid a finger on all those gifts before they were confiscated from us by the visiting area's corrupt watchdog.

We didn't talk about her time in a camp, or mine. Our deeply moving reunion was, like all those before it, made up of jokes, funny faces, carefree anecdotes, so carefree that for a moment I thought we were outside, in Karamay, Ürümqi, or Ghulja. I answered her with laughter. In each other's arms, we wept as well, my first tears in months. Tears of joy.

When Madina left the premises, I went back to my cell with a light heart. When one of the people you love most in all the world is suffering because of you, the guilt is crushing. But that was over now. She was free. In my mind, nothing else mattered.

The festivities began in late August. Streamers, Communist-red, spattered the room where, like the good little soldiers we'd been taught to imitate, we paraded around and then sang our lungs out. My cellmates and I didn't win the competition, but when the teachers passed out prizes to the winners, we all craned our necks to see. They were crates of donut peaches.

Madina's peaches.

11. Losing Body and Mind

20th November 2017

had been a prisoner in Xinjiang for a year. And for almost half that time, I'd been stuck in Baijiantan. My mother and sisters came back on 3rd October. Since then, I hadn't seen a single familiar face. I hoped nothing had happened to them. Prison had become my only reality. The only horizon I had was the line of barbed wire that cut us off from the rest of the world. Everything I'd known before – family, being a wife and a mother, France – floated around in my head like another woman's story. A woman I no longer was.

My health was deteriorating despite my diligence in maintaining my body, which was soft and sore from lack of exercise. I did stretches during brief respites in my cell, early in the morning and late at night. It's not that we were underfed; quite the opposite. But still, I was visibly losing weight. I think they put something in the food. There was something extra about its taste, its consistency, as if someone were sprinkling invisible seeds on our plate. Were they drugging our meals?

Maybe it was just time going by that wore me down, but I realised I was losing my memory. My thoughts would get tangled up like a ball of yarn.

In the daytime, our line of prisoners would drag themselves across the linoleum like a single big sleepwalker in blue pyjamas. Sometimes, one of us would faint. A guard would take her away and bring her back a few hours later. We barely even noticed. Plenty of things that we had once found shocking were now the norm. Slaps, insults, fellow prisoners getting heart attacks or just vanishing: all that was daily life here. The arduous pace of life in detention – with its succession of classes and meals that were just as hard to swallow – was so exhausting that I couldn't even think anymore. The teachers gave us each a diary. In the rare moments of 'free time' at our disposal, we were to write down our thoughts: our dreams, our memories, our 'sins.' Every three days, guards would collect these notebooks. Our teachers would read them over, worming their way into the troubled intimacy of our hearts. Did they really think I'd divulge the slightest truth in those pages? Writing gave me no solace because all those pages written in the pallid light were just lies. A smokescreen to fool my teachers and their destructive 're-education.' Inside, I laughed at those idiotic sentences. But deep down, I knew that the constant self-criticism I'd been reduced to was, with every passing day, moving me farther away from the Gulbahar I'd once been.

When Baijiantan slumbered, I remained awake. It was the only time I had to think. At night, eyes wide open in the dark, I prayed with all my strength: I am innocent. I am innocent. I am innocent.

Life changed at Baijiantan. It all began on 18th October, with the Nineteenth National Congress of the Communist Party. For three days, a wave of excitement had swept through the ranks – not only the guards and the teachers, but us as well. Xi Jinping was preparing to give his big speech to an audience of the nation's leaders, with an eye to being re-elected for a second five-year term. And we were going to watch him on TV, from our classroom. As in Uyghur households on the eve of Eid, the camp gave itself a thorough cleaning. Everything had to be impeccable.

The guards had always demonstrated a paranoid sense of hygiene. That was one of the first things I learned here: each detainee, each room had to be irreproachably spotless. Outside of class, we would be found on our knees, armed with soap and rags, sponging the floor. The slightest bit of dirt overlooked would be met with reprimand or punishment. Baijiantan had to be the very image of our obedient souls: the more it gleamed with unsettling cleanliness, the better our 're-education' was going.

But this time, we had to work twice as hard. Nothing was too good for the President of China. Big red-and-gold banners just like the Party's snaked across the walls. The teachers set up TV screens in every classroom. The closer we got to the 18th, the more our monotonous daily routine took on a new interest: some prophesied that Xi would hail the efficacy of programmes meant to combat terrorism, of which the 're-education' camps were the backbone. He might even ease up on the rules inside camps. Our living conditions might improve. The most exemplary among us might even enjoy the freedom we so longed for. Our hopes lent us energy as the camp dressed up in Communist colours. An air of celebration almost floated in the foul-smelling, windowless hallways. All this staging was, of course, part of our own 're-education.' We were tasked with retaining, from this moment of 'shared joy,' the greatness of our collective father. It was laughable. But short of being released – a pipe dream I'd buried in a corner of my mind – the prospect of seeing our living conditions get even a little bit nicer kept me from foundering completely.

And then the day came. On the morning of the 18th, we were all seated at our desks. We had even laundered our blue uniforms for the occasion. The scent of soap mingled with that of sweat in the room where the only light came from the flatscreen. Advertisements played on a loop. The tension rose. At last the live broadcast from Beijing began. Beneath the heavy crimson curtains of the Great Hall of the People, the President of the People's Republic of China strode to the podium to thunderous applause from his thousands of loyal supporters.

I'd seen the man before in photos, paintings, and on TV. But I'd never really given him a good look, or listened to what he had to say, because politics isn't really my thing. So this was Xi Jinping. Boxed in by the TV screen, this miniature version of him seemed harmless enough. His round face and black jacket buttoned up around a plump torso gave him a good-natured air. I remember his speech was very long and vehement. I also remember patriotic songs ringing out all over camp. The minute we were no longer riveted to our seats facing the screen, our teacher beat time and, at the top of our lungs, we sang of the glory of Xi and our great nation:

WITHOUT THE COMMUNIST PARTY, THERE WOULD BE NO NEW CHINA.
THE COMMUNIST PARTY TOILS FOR THE NATION.
THE COMMUNIST PARTY OF ONE HEART SAVED CHINA.

Above all, I remember that it was after his re-election that life in Baijiantan changed. But sadly, not in the ways we'd hoped.

The first thing they did was ban free time. Weekends did not exist here. We worked all week, from sunrise to sunset. Each day was exactly like the last; it had been that way for months. And yet, Saturdays and Sundays stood out, for though they had their share of chores and classes, on weekends guards let us out of our cells for a few hours at the end of the day. This reprieve didn't happen all the time. It depended on their mood. During these rare breaks, we got visits and or called on 'friends' from neighbouring cells. Sure, it was still life in prison, but it was a bit of life all the same.

I learned a great deal about the camps during these let-ups as the guards looked leniently on. Everywhere, conversations were abuzz over handfuls of dice or dog-eared decks of cards. While songs in Chinese rang out in the corridors, the latest lowdown on Baijiantan gleaned during the week made the rounds among us. Recently, one topic had dominated all discussion: vaccination. We had all been forcibly given injections.

One morning, our warders had led us one at a time into a makeshift infirmary where a small team of Hans in lab coats was waiting. I shouted and protested wholeheartedly for hours, but I was given no choice. 'You must be vaccinated, Gulbahar. You're 50 years old, your immune system isn't what it used to be. If you don't do this, you might get the flu. I'm getting a shot too, just like you,' said one of the superintendents as she pointed to the syringes and other paraphernalia sitting beside a medical exam table. From fear of reprisal, I signed a document giving my permission, then let one of the lab-coated men jab the vein in my arm. I was so stupid. Now I know that woman was lying. She told other detainees the same thing. But that's not even the worst of it. During our free time, many women confessed to me, ashamed, that they were no longer having their periods. They reported that their menstrual flow had stopped shortly after the 'vaccinations.' The younger women, most of whom were engaged to be wed, wept and grieved. They had hoped to start families once they were released from camp. Past the menopause myself, I tried to comfort them, though a horrific thought was already growing inside me: were they sterilising us?

Ever since the National Congress, we hadn't been allowed to smile at each other, or even exchange glances. 'Lower your head. Don't you know that looking at others is forbidden?' the guards shouted. If a line of prisoners passed by my own, I looked down and grew absorbed in studying my hideous black slippers. The same rules applied at the mess hall and the bathroom in the morning. Why strip us of our last remaining freedoms? Every day, new prisoners arrived at the camp. They filled the cells beside mine. I saw their fearful faces. I wanted to reach out and reassure them, shout 'Watch out! Don't get vaccinated!' But what was the point? Their turn would come, no matter what, and I'd just get punished. So I kept my mouth shut. There were more of us than ever at Baijiantan, and yet never had I felt so alone.

Something strange was brewing outside, I could feel it. The chaos of Xinjiang ricocheted off the walls of the camp, its distant echo making its way to our ears. The guards, more nervous now, mentioned official inspections. People from Ürümqi, local Party cadres, were soon coming to the camp to check on 'hygiene and the content of the instruction,' we were told. 'The best students will have to respond to their questions.' I was one of these. What a farce. A tissue of lies, those answers. We were ordered to learn them by heart. Were I asked for my opinion, I was to say: 'The training centre makes me very happy. I am being taught a trade and am very well fed. I am paid a small salary. I am provided with enough to feed and dress myself on a daily basis.' All this was untrue. We were given barely enough to clothe and bathe ourselves. The only thing we were even given here, day in and day out, was an earful about how Uyghurs were terrorists and should confess. Why were they ordering us to lie like this? Did they have something to hide?

Meanwhile, a few weeks after the famous Congress, we were each assigned an individual 'tutoress.' As if we weren't already bent double by the thick textbooks we had to learn by heart, sessions with these women further burdened our hellishly paced weekly schedules. Mine was named Mihray. I met her in a visiting room, where each time she sat waiting for me, my 'file' right under her nose. She was a young Uyghur woman with a mass of brown hair pulled back in a strict bun on the nape of her neck. Her gentle voice invited trust, so I told her about everything: my arrest, my family in France, my innocence. She besieged me with questions, and I did the same. 'When will I be released? May I see my family? May I call them, please?' Softly, sweetly, she would parry my demands: 'Patience, Gulbahar.' And yet, since the Congress, Mihray had been wary, weighing my words and reading in them potential evidence of insolence. Oh, the irony of fate: Mihray was the only person I had to talk to. The more we were muzzled, the more our sessions began to seem like police interrogations. When I asked here when I'd be able to leave this place, her face twisted in a pout of displeasure: 'Gulbahar, you must repent. You must confess. Why do you keep asking when you're getting out of here? How can I ever trust you? Who's to say that once you're released, you won't go back to your old ways?'

One day, as if to reward me, she finally said, 'You must wait for your trial.' My trial? Now, after months without a trace of a lawyer or even a charge, they were telling me I was going to be tried? At that moment, I gave up hope. After the trial, I would be sentenced, and it would all be over. My only outlet was prayer. God alone could hear me now. I had no idea what was going on outside, but my premonition proved to be right: something was going on. Every day brought with it a new minibus full of women. Baijiantan was now a factory swarming with hundreds of prisoners. Out there, Uyghurs were being arrested right and left. The police were racing against the clock, as if someone were trying to thwart their grand 're-educational' project. They were trying to make us disappear even faster than before. If we didn't die of exhaustion here, the 'trials' we were promised would be the end of us. Would they sentence me to death? I wasn't betting much on the life of a Uyghur woman who had fled to a foreign land.

Chapter 12

Nothing, but nothing, was happening anymore. Pure nothingness. In the deep midwinter of late 2017, I succumbed at Baijiantan. In the year that followed, I wasted away between the frozen walls of my cell, which filled with distraught women whose names had been replaced with numbers, whom I no longer had the strength to get to know. In the maze of the camp, cut off from the rest of the world, my perseverance crumbled away. The exhausting routine repeated itself infinitely, becoming one all-encompassing, gruelling day. Every day we submitted ourselves to the guards' whistles, shouts, and insults. In the foul-smelling corridors, our ghostly shadows trudged to the bathroom, then slogged to the classroom where we choked down the teachers' lies until evening fell. Sometimes, the screams of some women at night still woke others with a start. When these distant voices pierced the darkness, frigid figures sat up from their beds, then sank feebly back down into the dark. I opened an eye but no longer gave any thought to where the screams were coming from, or what tortures were being put to those victims. I fell back asleep.

An old idea came back to haunt me: I, Gulbahar Haitiwaji, was innocent. Once upon a time, I'd been a loving mother. A passionate wife. A woman who stood on her own two feet, upright and determined, a woman who was alive. My family and I had left Xinjiang, and France had given us freedom. I loved France, the land of 'the rights of man,' as Kerim never stopped repeating with the grateful pride of a man who had been given a new home. None of that had been so long ago. A year, maybe more, I'd lost track; time didn't exist anymore. The faces of Kerim, Gulhumar, and Gulnigar floated around in my unreliable mind. Memories slipped through my fingers like running water. I watched them go.

Absorbing lessons and regurgitating them conscripted my time and energy to such a degree that I no longer had any left to think for myself. 'You are criminals. Confess your crimes and the Party will pardon you. Then you will be freed,' we were told all day long. We buckled beneath the weight of this incessant refrain from teachers and warders. The relentless clockwork of brainwashing finally penetrated even the boldest and most impervious among us. 'Chen Quanguo is really underestimating us. He'll never change us, not like this,' one of my cellmates whispered one night. In the dark, her middle finger to Xinjiang's top official made me smile. I wanted to believe the Party hadn't won, but hadn't the 're-education' already worked?

'Criminals!' What was the point of bending over backwards protesting that you weren't? For a whole year, then, I fell silent. I feigned repentance during exchanges with my tutoress. For a while now, Mihray no longer bothered trying to sugarcoat our conversations in her dulcet tones. The young woman, herself the victim of potent brainwashing, had shown her true colours, giving me a glimpse of her work's hidden objective: extracting a confession. During our meetings, she'd repeat the same thing ten, 50, sometimes 100 times: my living nightmare would not come to an end until I confessed my crimes. I had to put it all out there at the trial. Beg the Party's forgiveness. Yes, there would be a trial, she assured me. She didn't know when. What would I be judged for, I who had been nothing but a mother, a wife, and an honest worker when I lived in Xinjiang? Would I have a right to a lawyer, when I'd been denied one for the entire time I spent in jail? Mihray claimed she knew nothing about the factors involved in the ruling. For a year, the thought of my trial haunted me. It became my obsession, my lifeline and my grave. I clung to it with stubborn resignation, convinced that no matter the sentence, it would be my only chance at escaping the hell that was Baijiantan.

❊ ❊ ❊

On the outside, in Xinjiang, the repression was speeding up. Women poured out of trucks by the dozen at Baijiantan. The aggressiveness on the part of teachers and guards, pressure from Mihray, and rising tensions in the camp hinted that China was in a race against time.

In Xinjiang, even those who weren't sent to the camps suffered at the hands of brutal police who held all the power. Regulations hailed down from major cities to the north and south. No beards, no headscarves, no giving your children Uyghur names, no using WhatsApp, no communicating with anyone abroad, no taking part in traditional religious ceremonies.... As the list got longer, the arbitrariness of a policy aimed at eradicating Islam and Uyghur culture showed through.

Under the guise of a massive public health programme, provincial authorities began collecting DNA, fingerprints, retinal scans, and blood types for millions of citizens. This was not a new undertaking, since the police were already collecting biometric data on those they deemed suspicious as part of the war against terrorism, starting with anyone who applied for a passport.

From now on, the people of Xinjiang were no longer citizens, but suspects. The massive stockpiling of DNA, carefully organised in the digital labyrinth where the police stored their files, confirmed a terrible theory: all citizens of the province, so long as they were Uyghur, represented a potential terrorist threat. No quarter would be afforded them. 'Show absolutely no mercy,' Xi Jinping told local Party cadres on a visit to Xinjiang in 2014, as revealed in documents leaked to the *New York Times*.

The repression pervaded even the remotest households with the 'Becoming Family' campaign. Party officials invited themselves over to the homes of Uyghur families for a week at a time, sharing their meals and sleeping under their roofs. Ordered to provide information about their personal lives and political views, Uyghurs were also subjected to a focused dose of barely disguised indoctrination in 'Xi Jinping Thought.' What happened to them after that? Were they spared a stay at a camp or otherwise rewarded if they docilely submitted to the cadres' insidious exercise? We had no idea. Those families that tried to share information, hiding behind assumed names, were swiftly silenced. No sooner were their first-hand accounts posted to Human Rights Watch and Amnesty International than they vanished into the Bermuda Triangle of Xinjiang.

In this way, Beijing was slowly stamping out the Uyghurs, sometimes with camps, sometimes with silence. But why had Xi suddenly decided to expand his 're-education' campaign beyond his 'schools'? How to explain the rush to wipe out the Uyghurs?

❊ ❊ ❊

In early 2018, a stunned world found out about the 'schools' in Xinjiang. Human rights organisations were no longer the only ones sounding the alarm. China's perfect surface, protected up till now by its Great Firewall, was cracking as scattered accounts from survivors started popping up in the press and images from whistleblowers made their way around the world, from Canada to China by way of the United States.

Members of the Uyghur diaspora were demonstrating in European capitals. Under the sky-blue flags of East Turkestan, they carried enlarged photos of loved ones who'd been missing for months or even years.

Under the leadership of the World Uyghur Congress, they begged governments around the world to act. Citizens on Chinese social networks who witnessed the atrocities being committed in Xinjiang took great risks in posting images and videos online. In Xi Jinping's China, a special fate was reserved for young Uyghur women. Several videos report communal wedding ceremonies where Uyghur women in traditional robes posed empty-eyed, lids heavy with mascara, on the arms of stylishly bedecked Han men, all smiles. These women were probably forced into marriage, but for now, there was no way to obtain tangible proof. Their voices could not be heard; they were prisoners of a Xinjiang that had been barricaded away. Were these marriages an alternative to camps? Were these sacrificial women being bartered to redeem the 'crimes' of their loved ones? Were they purchased by Hans, as is common with Vietnamese women in southern China? Uyghurs abroad seized upon these videos and passed them on, giving a glimpse of the many horrific stories that announced something no one wants to confront but we all must, head-on, because all the evidence points to it: genocide.

Western democracies that had been reluctant to pronounce on the subject for the last two years no longer had a choice: the suspicions weighing on China were now too numerous to be ignored, the accusations too serious. Washington soon took a stand on the front lines. For years, the US has been welcoming many political opponents, artists and intellectuals from Xinjiang, whose ranks included Rebiya Kadeer, the 'mother of Uyghurs.' Faced with the Chinese enemy, the political establishment has already made itself a megaphone for the cause. The ups and downs of 2018 gave the then US President, Donald Trump, an occasion to seize upon the 'Uyghur issue' once more and turn it to his own ends, like any other Sino-American difference of opinion – 5G, Hong Kong, Taiwan – as the latest spearhead in the trade war with Beijing.

But European democracies do not have the same stake in the game. They squirm, uneasy, for any such match seems stacked against them, not to say a foregone loss. First of all, because China excels in the domain of economic diplomacy: the money it lavishes, notably on European countries, buys indulgence and forces government concessions. China's final trump card boasts unusual dimensions: the 'New Silk Roads,' the vast infrastructure project China is developing on land and sea alike, with an eye toward linking the Middle Kingdom and Europe and inevitably designating the latter as one of its privileged commercial partners.

In addition, China is worming its way into gaps offered by the United Nations. In 2018, as the transformation of Xinjiang was steadily progressing, Beijing was scheming with the UN's subsidiary agencies to place its pawns in strategic positions. Its agents wielded lobbying and threats to achieve their ends, slowly specifying, little by little, new rules for the international game where human rights would be sidelined in favour of a country's social and economic development. China's voice already carried far more weight than its right of veto, again due to the money it injected into different levels of the UN. For example, two years earlier it created a Peace and Development Trust Fund through which it committed to financing projects to the tune of $200 million over the next ten years. Of the three organisations headed by Chinese Secretary Generals – international civil aviation, industrial development, and telecommunications –

the first two saw their incumbent Chinese directors have their terms renewed in 2018 for three and four years, respectively. Discreetly, China has been setting itself up in places of lasting strategic importance.

The best example of this no doubt remains the election of Qu Dongyu to the head of the Food and Agriculture Organisation (FAO), the specialised agency tasked with leading the fight against famine throughout the world. In July 2019, the Vice-Minister of the Ministry of Agriculture and Rural Affairs handily won the election by a landslide, with 108 out of 191 votes, although the French candidate, agricultural engineer Caroline Geslain-Lanéelle, was heavily favoured to win. Among the diplomatic ranks were murmurs that lobbying and Chinese money had carried the day once more: China, which had been copiously funding the FAO for years, was said to have wiped out the debt of several member nations, including Cameroon (to the tune of $70 million) in exchange for its candidate's withdrawal. After her campaign, Caroline Geslain-Lanéelle declared that 'China ran a highly aggressive campaign using means that we did not employ.'

Bringing all its weight to bear on the UN, China anticipated the accusations that would be made when the file on 're-education camps' in Xinjiang reached the discussion table before the UN Human Rights Council in Geneva, Switzerland. It conducts investigations and delivers reports on countries with a shaky human rights record. In 2018, a Uyghur file already existed, but did not lead to any confrontation with China.

❋ ❋ ❋

As I would learn later, my daughter Gulhumar's struggle was getting nowhere, far from the media spotlight and the knowing looks from UN experts. Even as revelations about the 're-education' camps came pouring in from all over, my daughter sent out messages in bottles to secure my release. She knocked on all the doors: those of Uyghur families living in exile, prominent figures of the diaspora, lawyers specialising in human rights. They showered her with advice and assurances, but got no results.

She wore herself out, with France's vice-consul in Beijing, in correspondence that got bogged down. Most of her desperate e-mails received no reply. Sometimes, a consular employee would call her back to reassure her, but no concrete information, no negotiation with authorities in Xinjiang gave her hope I would ever return. The few calls she'd made to my mother or sister in Xinjiang were vague and worrisome. 'Everything's fine,' they'd tell her. 'Yes, really, your mother's doing fine, don't worry.' The last time she'd managed to reach my mother, my mother had burst into tears and confessed everything: 'Please, I'm begging you, don't take this the wrong way, but stop calling us. They came and questioned us for a long time, everyone's traumatised. No one has any idea why we're being treated like this.'

I pictured policemen – maybe the same ones who were holding me captive – in my mother's kitchen in Ghulja, interrogating them while she served them tea. And my mother, sitting across from them, promising to tell them everything she knew.

Four days later, Gulhumar tried her luck again. In vain. After she dialled her grandmother, the line went dead. All of a sudden, as if it had been physically cut. As if the number had abruptly been wiped from existence.

For two years, my daughters and my husband imagined the worst. They believed me dead. Kerim lost 30kg (65 pounds) and sank deep into depression. He worked nonstop, but the gleam in his eye had gone out. In moments of confusion and turmoil, he'd plan ways to come to Xinjiang and find me.

13. France Discovers Gulbahar

Spring 2018

The two men were separated by hundreds of thousands of miles. Several decades, too. The first, in his forties, was an independent scholar in Germany. The second, in his twenties, was a student of Chinese descent studying law at the University of British Columbia in Vancouver. While the first was feeling Beijing's wrath for his research into Chinese repression in Tibet, the second was still living in relative anonymity. Neither Chinese authorities nor the pockets of Uyghur diaspora scattered around the world were aware of him. The first was Adrian Zenz. The second, Shawn Zhang.

These two men had one thing in common. In the spring of 2018, during the media outpouring of horrific although unverifiable accounts from Uyghur families whose loved ones had disappeared, as well as from a few rare survivors of the Chinese 'schools,' these two men brought governments and international organisations what was missing: evidence. Mountains of evidence.

Painstakingly combing through official documents from the province, calls for construction bids from the public sector, and online job ads, Zenz traced the genesis of the 're-education' system. He was able to prove that the number of camps had multiplied since Chen Quanguo assumed leadership in Xinjiang, from August 2016 to spring 2018. He also dissected the local and regional press, where officials expressed themselves. His estimates were terrifying. According to Zenz, there were 1,200 're-education' centres in Xinjiang, each able to host an average of 250 to 880 internees. It was possible a total of just over one million people had been transported to these facilities.

Had China been caught at its own game due to negligence on the part of its mighty censorship machine? For over the course of his investigation, Zenz had accessed the data he needed without difficulty. Indeed, he'd only had to browse the province's sites, chock full of the boundless manna of incriminating information, to grasp the workings of the ideological 're-education' project targeting Uyghurs. Online, the Propaganda Department seemed unconcerned about covering up the instances of the words 're-education camp' and 'reform through labour' that speckled its listings. It was as if, behind Xinjiang's closed doors, these schools were an open secret.

In May 2017, for example, Karamay's public employment service put out an ad for '110 re-education centre staff for four different "centralised transformation through education classes",' as well as '248 police officers for police stations, checkpoints and "transformation through education bases", wrote Zenz. Shortly thereafter, two counties in Hotan Prefecture advertised 'several "transformation through education centre" teaching positions.' Requirements included 'knowledge in... criminal psychology' and 'Marxism.' The majority of construction bids stipulated facility standards that left no room for doubt, mentioning not only 'surrounding walls, security fences, wire mesh, barbed wire, reinforced security doors and windows,' but also 'surveillance systems, secure access systems, watchtowers, guard rooms, police stations or facilities for armed police forces,' and 'special doors and beds for prison cell use.' Such elements proved that these 'schools' were no mere schools, but genuine detention centres, fortified and highly securitised.

Meanwhile, Shawn Zhang was scrutinising satellite images. The geographic data specified in the calls for bids enabled him to locate dozens of camps. They were recognisable from their thick forests of barbed wire and the watchtowers bristling from the sides of buildings. Sometimes, where there had been nothing but a stretch of desert months before, he saw a gargantuan detention complex sprout from the very earth. Day after day, he pored over these images where camps were springing up overnight. He began blogging on the site Medium in spring 2018, offering information and screen captures of the first three centres located around Kashgar, Xinjiang's major southern city. The first post was dated 20th May 2018. Two days later, he published another: this time, a camp in Hotan. Then another the same day, traced to Karakax, another county in Hotan prefecture. The red markers multiplied on his interactive map. By becoming a whistleblower,

Zhang knew he was putting his family in China in danger. The Communist Party would not forgive him for giving the camps a face. Local authorities had already contacted his parents, but he continued to tirelessly update his blog.

If the world had still been in doubt, here was confirmation: China, despite all its claims, was not done with labour camps. Up until 2013, when it declared that it had abolished all such repressive methods from its penal system, China possessed a robust network of detention centres where it sent political and religious dissidents, criminals, and fringe elements of society without making much of a distinction. Established by Mao Zedong in 1957, the *laogai* (literally, 'reform through labour') were to the Middle Kingdom what the gulag had been to Russia: a gargantuan archipelago scattered throughout the land, where detainees exhausted themselves trying to redeem their 'crimes' by the sweat of their brow. A particularity of China's sprawling penal system was the independent category of *laojiao*, or 're-education through labour,' which unlike the *laogai* were not subject to the rules governing judiciary procedures in China. In other words, anyone could be sent to a *laojiao* for up to four years without a trial if their thoughts were deemed inappropriate. Supposedly abolished along with the *laogai* in 2013, these institutions were aimed at rehabilitating those the Party saw as having spiritual influences.

In many respects, the extra-judicial structure and ideological aims of these 'schools' resurrect the violent *laojiao* of the Maoist era. In Xinjiang, the repression does not target only the actions of Uyghurs, even if Beijing claims that such centres are a response to terrorist threats in the province. On several occasions, Zenz notes in the regional and local press that the Party, which liberally sprinkles its official declarations with medical terms, is attacking Uyghur thoughts and beliefs. According to the Communist Party, Uyghurs live in the toxic grip of religion, a disease that must be eradicated through 're-education.' They are a fertile breeding ground for radical Islam and terrorism, a plague that must be eradicated. Thus, the work of 're-education' camps focuses less on physical labour than transformation of the soul through techniques of exhaustion.

❅ ❅ ❅

Zenz and Zhang weren't the only ones rummaging through China's files in the spring of 2018. In Paris, in complete and utter anonymity, my daughter Gulhumar was also conducting her investigation. Thanks to her mastery of Mandarin, she was tirelessly scrutinising the Chinese internet for proof of the camps' existence. On apps like WeChat and Douyin, the equivalents of WhatsApp and TikTok, she compiled the posts of people she knew who'd stayed behind in Xinjiang. She had to be fast about it: most of these only remained online for a handful of minutes before the propaganda machine steamrollered right over them. So she saved everything that seemed suspicious to her: a job listing for workers in a 'school,' another for an electrician in a 'vocational training centre,' images of crematoriums, the empty streets of a once bustling neighbourhood in Karamay.... Her press clippings and desperate messages to the French embassy in Beijing hadn't been enough. She wanted to understand why our family in Xinjiang was no longer answering the phone.

For two years, while I'd been wasting away in Chinese detainment, she worked like a fiend for my survival and release. She knew the information she was after was highly confidential, somewhere deep in a secret database itself buried deep in the maze of files belonging to the authorities in Xinjiang. My file was one of those sensitive cases the authorities had hidden away. Xinjiang is a safe with no combination.

※ ※ ※

Winter, 2017: my file ended up at the French Foreign Ministry in Paris. An acquaintance had put Gulhumar in touch with the Ambassador for Human Rights there, François Croquette. He devoted an entire morning to hearing them out, her and four other Uyghurs living in exile. Thanks to him, there was now a 'consular' file in my name. Gulhumar was promised that my case would be treated as if I were a citizen of France.

From then on, a brown-haired woman in a dark suit that seemed to swallow her up saw Gulhumar once a month. In an unadorned office awash in light, Gulhumar told the woman about everything: our past in Karamay, our arrival in France, the peaceful years in Boulogne, and then that sudden, mysterious phone call, my departure, and my disappearance into the depths of Xinjiang.

She also confided her theory that I'd been locked up in a 're-education' camp, and her main fear: that Chinese authorities would sentence me to death. The woman across from her listened attentively, without interrupting. She took notes and, from time to time, passed Gulhumar a glass of water and let her catch her breath. When her voice grew choked with emotion, the woman leaned across the desk between them and gently pressed her hand.

On the ground in Beijing, the Foreign Ministry set its machine in motion. The team there contacted the French Embassy and China's Ministry of Foreign Affairs. Negotiations began. At this stage, it was more about figuring out where I was and why I was being held. Every month, a general meeting took place between the Embassy and Chinese authorities, at which my name was brought up. But for now, nothing conclusive had emerged from these discussions: the Chinese were content to take notes, the young woman in the dark suit told Gulhumar. 'Take notes? What do you mean, they're taking notes?' 'Well,' she explained, 'they're taking down information about your mother so they can pass it to their superiors.' Gulhumar suppressed her rage. The woman assured her that at every session, every summit, every private meeting between French leaders and their Chinese counterparts, my story was being mentioned. 'We're doing everything we can to get her out of there, I promise.'

No one in the inner workings of Franco-Chinese diplomacy was unaware of my case. The 'Gulbahar Haitiwaji affair': a Uyghur woman living in exile in France, being held by China for no reason in a secret government 're-education' camp. For the nth time, my daughter was asked to be patient. The negotiations under way were highly sensitive. A single misspoken word could offend China and close the case right away. Xinjiang was thousands of miles from Beijing. It was a place cut off from the world. So for now, asking the Chinese to send a delegation to the province was out of the question.

Gulhumar sighed. Our family had so little time left. Soon I'd have been locked up in Xinjiang for two years. At the same time as her meetings at the Ministry, Gulhumar was notifying the media. The young woman in her dark suit had given her permission. Surely by detailing her struggle to the press, she would reach more people with her story. But take care, the woman warned her, not to present me as a 'spokesperson' for the Uyghur cause or any political issue. That could harm what little progress we've made in the shadows. The Chinese would grow cold.

When Gulhumar came home at night, worn out from her busy days, doubt would set in once more. Was all this in vain? Kerim couldn't take it anymore. He grew enraged: 'If they're not going, then I'll go! I don't give a damn, I'm a political refugee! At worst, they'll lock me up in her place. She didn't do anything, damn it!' The press coverage and the meetings at the Ministry weren't enough for him. Gulhumar feared he would put his plan in action. What would she and Gulnigar do if he, too, left for Xinjiang?

❊ ❊ ❊

A few months later, a major event brought a breath of fresh air to the struggle. In August 2018, the UN officially denounced Xinjiang's 're-education' camps. This was the first time the institution had taken a stand. It was unprecedented, and the young woman in the dark suit called Gulhumar straightaway.

'This is going to get things moving. Keep the faith! We're making progress!' she exclaimed. Armed with Adrian Zenz's findings, Shawn Zhang's images, and the many accounts of Uyghurs living in exile, the UN intended to hold China accountable and establish an independent fact-finding mission to Xinjiang to take stock of the scope of what was no less than genocide.

China abruptly broke its silence. In October 2018, it acknowledged the existence of centres for 'transformation through education,' but rejected wholesale the accusation that these camps violated human rights , claiming instead that these were ordinary 'vocational training centres' aimed at fighting terrorism, Islam extremism, and unemployment. This reaction, as unsurprising as it was disturbing, confirmed what foreign observers had already been fearing: that China in no way intended to stop sending Uyghurs to penal colonies thinly disguised as 're-education' facilities. Indeed, quite the opposite. Its announcement in fact demonstrated that in 2018, it had perfected a legal system allowing it to justify the existence of its camps to the rest of the world.

14. Moved to a Bigger Camp

Somewhere in northern Xinjiang
5th November 2018

'Don't worry. You will all be tried for a specific crime.' The superintendent of Baijiantan meant these words to be reassuring. As if he were offering us a flower, presenting us poor little tired detainees with a gift. 'Here you go – prison for six, nine, or even 15 years! Just for you!' What a joke. Next thing we knew, he'd be forcing us to thank him. Six months ago, I'd been dumbstruck by something else I'd overheard the superintendent murmur: How could they try me if they didn't have anything on me? No wait, they did have something, a photo of Gulhumar at a protest in Paris, but that was all. Could a sentence be based on so little? I'd carefully refrained from putting that question to Mihray. I'd quit provoking people because punishments came raining down on us at the drop of a hat. At best the warders would've hit me a few times, at worst I'd have spent a week in solitary. I couldn't face either.

I was a shadow of myself now. A ghost.

If Kerim, Gulhumar, or Gulnigar saw me, they'd scream with fright. I weighed no more than 50kg(110 pounds). The blinding light of Baijiantan had worsened my vision, and beneath my eyes, heavy rings made two pockets of shadow. Once I had taken such care that not a single grey hair showed in my shock of hair. Now I found myself with a shapeless mass of tangled locks. My heart beat so weakly that I could no longer feel it when I pressed my palm to my chest. Sometimes, I'd throw my back out and my legs would stiffen like boards, abruptly shot through with unbearable cramps.

Everywhere around me, life in camp had left its indelible traces. By dint of dragging ourselves back and forth down these linoleum halls, we had become a pitiful heap of sagging, warped flesh. Our faces were greenish and swollen. Was it all the time spent inactive and sweating in that pallid fluorescence? I missed the light of day. We were only allowed three or four short walks a week. Was it the awful slop that filled our bowls? I barely touched it anymore. Had they left us here to die? If so, why bother feeding us? Or was it the shots they'd inflicted on us? In the spring, the nurses had claimed there was another flu epidemic. This time, I hadn't bothered with the fierce fight I'd put up the winter before. Like everyone else, I stuck out my arm for the nurse, then signed the release in Mandarin that she gave me. Like everyone else, I no longer had the courage at that moment to wonder if they were injecting us with a vaccine or some kind of poison that leached away our memories. For we were all losing our memories.

What would we become without our memories? At night, the whisperings of women had once wallpapered our cell. Our conversations inhabited it, making the malodorous place less squalid, less lonely. Mothers spoke of their children: an unruly youngest son, an eldest about to wed, a husband locked away in another camp, a men's camp. Young women smiled as they recalled their fiancés waiting for them on the outside, worrying if they'd be able to be 'normal' women after this – that is, with fulfilling family lives – something to which we older women brought our share of comfort and reassurance. I, for one, told them of life abroad: Uyghur families living in exile in a bungalow in the Paris suburbs gathering around a barbecue to celebrate the spring festival of Nowruz, the small solidarities that forged strong bonds, children who, as they grew, came to address each other in a foreign tongue. The others took it all in greedily but not without fear. Foreign lands. The rest of the world. It all seemed so far away.

Every night, these recollections had brought us back to life. Recounting them like spinning tales by the fireside fanned the embers of our memory. In this way, we remained the women we had been: mothers, wives, sisters. Even imprisoned, demeaned, I was still Gulbahar Haitiwaji, for my memories were my own. I would tell myself then that no one could ever take them away from me.

When our memories fled, so did our conversations. After our daily eleven hours of class, we would go back to our cells and slump onto our straw mattresses without a word. We no longer had the strength to revive, day after day, the happiness they had confiscated from us. Sometimes I still made a stab at a few yoga moves. Then I went to bed. In the suffocating silence, all that could be heard was the hiccup of the two-way AC in the wall.

Without our memories, we were nothing more than prisoners now. Women without names, without stories. 'Terrorists,' 'criminals,' just like they said. Without our memories, we were like the dead.

The more I think about it, the more I think that killing me would not have been beyond them. After all, China had already proven it had no scruples about the Uyghurs. I'd been here for almost two years, yet I was innocent. I'd seen dozens of women disappear, and I was being promised a trial that would send me who knew where – so why not a grave?

Starting this morning, the warders had put the superintendent's promise into practice. The first women were called up. They left the classroom in groups of two or three. The ones who left never came back. Where were they being taken? Prison? The middle of the desert, to be killed? Were other camps even more inhuman than our own?

By this time, I and the others were no longer in Baijiantan. We had been transferred last month. One night, after dinner, the warders led us not to the usual study hall but instead toward our cells without a world. They gave us each big black plastic trash bags. 'Gather your things,' they commanded. By the time they came back for us, it was late. They wrote our numbers on each bag and then took them all away. 'Where are we going?' one of the girls asked. 'Another camp. This one's too small. There's more space there. It's really big.' No one blinked an eye. It was late, almost one in the morning. I remember, because on the way there (a road I'd never been on before), we passed a clock. We were silently herded down a stairwell, and then we reached a soulless tiled room that reeked of fresh paint. A row of warders was waiting for us.

My stomach clenched so hard I thought I was going to throw up. What did they mean, take your clothes off? Here, in front of everyone, under these fluorescent lights? What were they going to do to us? 'Take your clothes off,' the lead warder repeated. We exchanged a few terrified glances out of the corners of our eyes. But what choice did we have? I began tugging slowly on the rusty zipper of my jumpsuit, then shuffled it down to my ankles. No one dared look at anyone else. It was a horrible moment. Figures passed behind our naked bodies, legs spread wide, stiff from the squatting position we'd been ordered to maintain. They checked to make sure we hadn't hidden anything in our private parts. I was bent forward, blood rushing to my head. I could feel moist exhalations on my back. I shut my eyes, disgusted, humiliated. Defiled.

We put our clothes back on. Our heads vanished into black burlap hoods, hands cuffed behind our backs. Then they had us all climb into trucks. Fifteen minutes later, we reached a place that looked like Baijiantan after an enlarging spell. The sameness was unsettling: the buildings, the hallways, the stairways, the cells.... They all looked completely identical, but compared to Baijiantan, the proportions of this place were gigantic. There were more than 500 women here.

A guard put an electronic bracelet around my wrist. The device pinched the skin beneath it and gave me an unpleasant sensation, as if my arm were numb and heavy from poor circulation. The cycle of classes, meals, and questioning resumed. Today they cálled up Nurgul, Gulmira, and Maynur.

I hoped they wouldn't tell me my trial date in advance. I hoped they would come and get me on the day. I didn't want to know when my turn would come. 'Don't be frightened. These trials are mere formalities,' the teachers told us. 'Count yourselves lucky. If you weren't in a camp, you'd be in prison.' The more they told us not to be afraid, the more I trembled with fear. I was deeply afraid.

15. 'No 9. Your Turn!'

23rd November 2018

This morning, the police burst into our classroom. 'Number 9? Your turn!' Shivering uncontrollably, I followed them through a series of hallways, security gates, more hallways and stairs. Once again, I was surprised by the sheer size of the camp. The guard's fingers blazed through codes on the keypads. He slapped his badge brusquely on the reader beside each door. In a sequence of beeps and clackings of automated gates, our little group was ushered from the building. It was the first time I'd breathed in the cold air. Freezing. My head spun.

Naïvely, I'd thought we were headed for the court in Karamay. This 'court' was instead located in a big rectangular building parallel to ours. We walked for a few minutes, giving me time to commit a few images to memory as we crossed over: the wall of electrified barbed wire that would fry anyone alive, several watchtowers, a well-kept lawn.

In the 'waiting room,' three other girls with terrified faces awaited in silence. My tutoress – not Mihray now, but a Mongolian woman – was expecting me. I watched her out of the corner of an eye. She didn't return my glances. I felt a foolish surge of hope: maybe she'd be defending my case before the judge? Maybe she'd tell him about my good grades. My obedient behaviour.

I joined the other defendants on the sofa. Someone handed me a glass of water. I gulped some into my dry mouth. Then, before I had time to think, a guard grabbed me by the shoulder and pushed me towards the hallway. The three other girls were ahead of me. Our tutoresses followed behind. A few minutes later, we were seated on a black bench, hands cuffed. Behind us, the teachers and a handful of visitors had come in. I spotted my sister: her moist eyes met my own. Madina! The authorities had told me she was coming. She'd made the trip from Ürümqi and there was sadness in her eyes. She took stock of me: prematurely aged, my face sickly, my dirty jumpsuit loose on my frame. I felt so pitiful about the situation that I couldn't bring myself to smile. My mouth twisted into a strange pout. The judge stated the name of the first woman and bade her stand. Muffled coughs, chairs scraping on the floor, the rustle of paper as the judge leafed through case files on the accused. The trial was under way.

The drawback of being last was having time for the certainty that I would end my days here to grow inside me. I was going to die in a camp. Thus preoccupied, I didn't catch any details of the verdicts before mine. I heard the plaintive voices of the women, their stammering attempts to provide explanation, the judge's severe tones as he dissected their lives. The ordinary lives of these ordinary women. But when these words reached my mind, they bounced right off. I couldn't understand them. Inside and outside, I was trembling all over. All I could remember was that the first two women were exonerated. The third received three years of 're-education.' And then, just like in a play, it was my turn to be in the spotlight. My nervousness evaporated when my name was called. I felt nothing. Nothing at all anymore. My body was stiff and hard as a wooden plank. The judge's words rebounded from it like balls.

❈ ❈ ❈

'The accused: Gulbahar Haitiwaji, 52 years of age, born 24th December, 1966 in Ghulja. She left Xinjiang for France in 2006. She has been married to Kerim Haitiwaji since 11th June, 1990. Kerim Haitiwaji is a political refugee in France and participates in the activities of the France Uyghur Association, a separatist and terrorist organisation. In 2006, Gulbahar Haitiwaji sold the apartment she owned with Kerim Haitiwaji in Karamay. That same year, she had the *hukous* of four family members annulled from records of the household: Kerim Haitiwaji, Gulhumar Haitiwaji, Gulnigar Haitiwaji, and herself.'

The judge cleared his throat and motioned for me to stand. I obeyed. I was no longer trembling. He said: 'Gulbahar Haitiwaji, do you recognise your daughter in this photo?' He then held up, for all to see, the snapshot of Gulhumar waving her blue flag at the Trocadéro. His voice rang out through the large hall. Its tiled floor was stocked with black plastic benches and a dais from which he and two other men looked down upon me. He wasn't wearing the robe I'd pictured, but instead, grey fatigues like a soldier. I answered him loudly and clearly: 'Yes, that is my daughter.' Then one of the three men said, 'Gulbahar Haitiwaji, in light of your actions, it would seem you have little consideration for your country.'

I didn't know what to say. The judge's voice was stern and solemn. My throat was tight. I lowered my head. On the bench behind me, my sister stifled a sob. I turned around to ask her to be quiet.

❉ ❉ ❉

None of this remotely resembled a trial. A trial has a courtroom that looks like a courtroom, not some interrogation room in a police station; a judge that looks like a judge, not someone in a military uniform like the pudgy little man before me. Real, actual people sit on the benches, people closely or distantly related to the accused: family, friends, colleagues. They are called to the stand to bear witness. Here, the black plastic benches were empty, and there was no witness stand. My sister blew her nose in a corner of the room, and apart from her exasperating sniffles, the only thing we heard from her were her thanks to the judge and the Chinese Communist Party for 'giving me the opportunity to show remorse,' after my sentence was pronounced. Of course, someone had fed her this little speech. A cameraman was filming the whole thing.

Another feature of a normal trial is an attorney representing the accused. They intercede between judges and clients to defend the latter, a shield against the judicial apparatus arrayed against them. The only person sitting beside me was my tutoress, her face unreadable, her lips pressed tight. In the whole nine minutes of my trial, she didn't speak once. A real trial has a defendant with actual accusations levelled against them – that is, someone who's done something worthy of being judged and, if convicted, sentenced. Me? I was innocent.

No, this trial wasn't a trial at all, of course, but everyone acted like it was: the soldier-judge, his flunkies to his right and left (policemen in uniform), the tutoresses who should have leapt at the chance to play lawyer, raising an eyebrow when the judge spoke, replying to their clients' worried gazes with a polite smile. And we four, the accused, trapped in a Kafkaesque, illegal judicial system where there was no such thing as justice and no way that we were going to be judged for what we had done, but rather automatically condemned for who we were: Uyghurs.

More even than Kerim's activism in France or the photo of Gulhumar, the elements in my case file that gave the judge the most trouble were the annulled *hukou* and the sale of our Karamay apartment. 'Why did you have the names removed for yourself, your daughters, and your husband?' he persisted. 'As I told you before, we left for France because my husband had a job offer there. I annulled three *hukou* – for my husband and my two daughters – not four. Yes, my husband applied for and obtained political asylum.' Instead of asking me why we'd decided to move abroad, which had been the main accusation for the last two years, the judge turned to attacking the apartment.

'You sold it in 2006, is that correct?'

'No, in 2010. We had already resettled in France at the time.'

Then something strange happened. The judge repeated his question, as if he hadn't registered my explanation. Or as if he'd wanted to spend the precious minutes correcting administrative errors because, as I was now convinced, my sentence had been decided beforehand.

All the Uyghurs being judged had some connection to a foreign country, often in Europe. Some made frequent phone calls to a brother, a sister, one of their children living in exile. Others even wired money. I was the only one who'd chosen to live in exile myself. Each of them had been sentenced to six, seven, or eight years of 're-education.'

The judge would not let go. 'You annulled three *hukou*, or four? And the apartment – you sold it in 2006?'

As I've said, three hukou. For my two daughters, and my husband. My husband is the only one to obtain asylum status. I did not seek naturalisation. No, the apartment was sold in 2010.

Nothing I could have said would've altered the results of this sham trial. The discussion dwelt on a few more administrative banalities, and then the judge left me a minute to express my 'regrets.' My sister had stopped sobbing, and there was not a sound in the room to interrupt that declaration that came pouring forth – with, I must admit, no small measure of hypocrisy. Deep down, all my sickened, outraged being was howling. But outside, it was vital to fake repentance, pull the wool over their eyes.

I said: 'I made certain administrative mistakes because I was ignorant of the law. I promise I'll never do it again. Though I have lived in France for ten years, I've never stopped loving China. That is in fact why I have never sought naturalisation. In my heart of hearts, I will always love China.'

'I hope you will continue to do so,' the man to the judge's left replied. Then the verdict was pronounced. I was reminded that I ought to feel lucky, that my crimes were worthy of prison and that, in its largesse, the court of Xinjiang was sending me to a better place: a school where I could learn and serve out my sentence in respectable living conditions. No, I might not serve out my entire term; that depended on me, my behaviour, the searching introspection I would perform, the energy I put into redeeming my crimes. But I'd already stopped listening. My ears were buzzing, everything was spinning, the whole world had been reduced to two words: seven years. Seven years.

❀❀❀

The trial was over. Night had fallen. In my new cell – the only thing 'new' about it was that it was located in the building next to the one where I'd been kept – girls who had been sentenced like me huddled up close to each other to hear the story of my 'trial.' Once out of the hearing chamber, two warders had me wait in a room with a large picture window that looked out on a hallway. Next door was a mess hall and as I was trying to picture the broad strokes of my life for the next seven years, I heard the squeak of slippers from the hallway.

The women lined up along the window in single file. There were Nurgul, Gulmira, and Maynur, the girls who'd been taken away for their trials a few days ago, whom I hadn't seen since.

We were in the building for those who had been tried. Their eyes filled with concerned curiosity, the girls asked me silent questions. I could read their lips. 'How many years? How many years did they give you?' I held up seven fingers. 'Seven years?' Yes, seven. The girls found that 'heavy.' I insisted with my hands. We laughed. In such terrible moments, you don't know what to think or feel. So laughter comes bubbling up like a breath of fresh air.

16. Where is Gulbahar?

19th February 2019
Paris

Her voice was clear and careful, her face sombre and impassive, her answers precise. That night, Gulhumar was sitting across from a blonde reporter. In her black sweater, her features worn by worry, my daughter looked like she was in mourning. She was a guest on *France 24* news. It was late winter 2019, and Paris was bone-chillingly cold. As the French were reeling from the shockwave of the *gilets jaunes* protesters, Gulhumar was entering the key phase of her struggle.

She addressed China openly, without mincing words: 'I demand the release of my mother Gulbahar, an innocent woman.' This was a first in the European Uyghur diaspora, a bomb lobbed at China. Behind her, the giant screen that curved around the stage displayed the faces of her parents and sister, all smiles, in the Hall of Mirrors at the Château de Versailles, before the moats of Chenonceau in the Loire, in front of the rides at Disneyland Paris. At her wedding in August 2016, too. An eternity ago. While the photos and memories paraded past, Gulhumar told the story of how I'd been trapped by the Chinese system.

It had all begun two years ago. I, Gulbahar had vanished overnight while on a two-week trip to Karamay, in Xinjiang. Since then, I hadn't been able to send word or even an image to my family to tell them I was still alive. My husband and daughters lived in worry. Always on the phone, they'd managed over the course of a few months to get through to our families in Altay and Ghulja, friends in Ürümqi and Karamay. No one knew a thing. If they picked up once, they never called back.

At the same time, they also alerted national authorities. In Beijing, the consular services were feeling their way along. Xinjiang had become a locked room no foreign delegation could access. So far, all negotiations had come to nothing. Gulhumar had even launched into a long e-mail exchange with the vice-consul, to no avail. In Paris, my file had gone from the consulate's hands to those of the Foreign Minister. Again in vain.

I had well and truly disappeared, and none of the competent authorities could locate where the police were detaining me. My family was absolutely convinced I was being held against my will in Xinjiang. I had left the region 13 years ago and was married to an asylee in France, so I was a choice target for the Communist Party. Teams of diplomats who were busy in the shadows showered my family in France with advice and reassurance, but they weren't turning up any serious leads. Until June 2017, when a neighbour in

Karamay finally picked up. 'Your mother is at a school. She's doing fine,' she whispered to Gulhumar over the phone.

The worst-case scenario had been confirmed. It was now clear I was undergoing 're-education.' In Europe and the United States, Uyghur organisations representing the diaspora were screaming ethnic and cultural genocide. Protests were on the rise to denounce Beijing's repression of their own people, backed up by proof. Online, the Xinjiang Victims Database, maintained by people of the diaspora, attempted to record everyone who had been sucked into the camps. The site displayed photos of missing individuals beside the date of their disappearance and the reason for their detention, such as:

Name: Alim Sulayman
Number: 4014
Age: 34
Gender: male
Profession: medicine
When problems started: before 2017
Status: sentenced (17 years)
Detention Reason (suspected/official): related to going abroad

Name: Shadiye Zakir
Number: 1597
Age: 57
Gender: female
Profession: energy
When problems started: Jan 2018 – Mar. 2018

Status: sentenced (7 years)

Detention Reason (suspected/official): related to going abroad

Name: Minewer Tursun

Number: 1601

Age: 53-54

Gender: female

Profession: housemaker

When problems started: Oct. 2017 – Dec. 2017

Status: unclear (soft)

Detention Reason (suspected/official): contact with outside world

Name: Qonai Qasymhan

Number: 2444

Age: 42

Gender: male

Profession: private business

When problems started: –

Status: sentenced (2018, 14 years)

Detention Reason (suspected/official): related to religion | 'terrorism,' 'extremism'

To further illustrate what had befallen me, Gulhumar invoked the stories of two survivors, both refugees now, one in the U.S. and one in Turkey. Their accounts beggar belief: nights spent keeping watching in turns over cells they shared with 40 other women. The tasteless food, the mysterious medication that plunged inmates into a state of torpor where memories frayed and time disappeared, along with menstrual cycles. Electric shocks administered through special helmets.

But that night on *France 24*, there was one thing Gulhumar didn't talk about: the apartment in Boulogne and the atmosphere of misery that reigned there. Books now sat on shelves under a thick layer of dust in a living room that had once been spotless. Kerim paced in circles when he wasn't flicking nervously at his iPad for the latest news from Xinjiang. He was smoking nonstop. The Winston butts piled up in the ashtray by the neglected windowboxes. Gulnigar had shut herself away in her room, her face buried in her pillow or her phone.

Since my disappearance, my eldest daughter Gulhumar had been keeping house. She stopped by three days a week after work, planning meals, stocking the freezer, feather-dusting the furniture. Sometimes, she didn't have the courage to face opening certain rooms left in darkness. The chaos inside was too great, like the turmoil in her heart. At night, she went home, exhausted, to the apartment in Nanterre she shared with her husband, Kaiser. There she would explode, howling out the pain she felt, then fall asleep, her face bathed in tears. But every morning, anger was what woke her up – that Kazakh anger in her, as her grandmother in Altay always put it. That temper I knew so well.

❉ ❉ ❉

In late February 2019, Gulhumar's appearance on *France 24* went largely unnoticed by the greater public. But for Uyghurs in France, a low-profile community of mostly students, it was like a shockwave. Half-riveted, half-terrified, they shared the video on social networks. It was an unexpected breath of fresh air; for months now, they had been receiving numerous text messages and calls from unlisted numbers based in China. These messages were coming from police stations in Xinjiang, dictated by intelligence services and typed by officials tasked with keeping tabs on and track of Uyghurs who'd fled abroad.' They sought to repatriate these 'traitors'; the same fate that had befallen me awaited them.

Requests for documentation came flooding in, each finickier and more oppressive than the last, from copies of leases to proof of enrolment in classes to diplomas. So did summonses, for when a student took the bait, the unnamed agent on the other end grew dogged. Students saw themselves ordered to participate in France Uyghur Association events and then to report on the goings-on. Or to get close to a prominent activist in the community. In short, to spy for China, with financial aid for the most cooperative, since students were always short of money. Under the cover of 'promoting ethnic minorities abroad,' the Embassy passed out scholarships. This fooled no one in the community. Recipients of these scholarships slept poorly. You had to tread carefully.

And if the students refused? Chinese spies fell back on blunt-force persuasion: weren't their families still back in Xinjiang, within the authorities' reach? Should the text message from an unlisted number go unanswered for several days, it would be reinforced by a second message, from a loved one. 'Please do what they want.' This injunction, written out like a last will and testament, almost always obtained the desired result. The students obeyed. They discreetly informed on others.

For a few months, the Embassy had been secretly hatching a new scheme meant to make the most defiant Uyghurs abroad give in. Those who applied to have their passports renewed would be categorically turned down, with no reason given. 'You're from Xinjiang. We cannot renew your passport. You must return home to start the application process. That's the new policy,' they were told at the service window in Paris. Without a passport, there was no way to secure the precious residence permit that allowed them to pursue their studies in France. A Sword of Damocles was dangling over their heads. By dooming them to be undocumented, the Embassy was forcing them to return to Xinjiang. Again, this fooled no one: it was obvious that once there, they would be locked up in camps.

❊ ❊ ❊

That night, then, in the climate of mistrust where it was hard to tell friend from informer, Gulhumar's words proved a balm for Uyghurs in France being hunted from Beijing. To all those students whose anonymous accounts in the press told of fear, she gave courage. My daughter didn't know it yet, but when she walked off the stage at *France 24*, she'd just kicked off hostilities. She'd openly accused China of inhuman treatment. She was the first collateral victim of the repressive measures in Xinjiang to do so. The consequences were commensurate with the risks she'd taken: enormous. Behind her, in the shadows, the Foreign

Ministry waited for retaliation. Xi Jinping's meeting with Emmanuel Macron in Paris was set for the next month. It would prove decisive.

17. Letting Myself Die

3rd March 2019
Karamay

I was going to spend the next seven years here. Not that I'd given into the idea, but I had no choice but to surrender to the life that was resuming its usual course. A string of identical days paraded by, without morning or night, sadness or hope. There was no such thing as Monday, or Tuesday or Friday; no lunch or dinner; no lessons any different from the ones that had come before. There were only days devoid of meaning, where the echo of my fellow detainees chewing in the mess hall gave way to the warders' shouts, which in turn gave way to the teachers' litanies of propaganda. My birthday, 24th December, was coming up, but far from rejoicing, I consoled myself with the prospect of a visit from my mother and sister: I'd managed to negotiate an hour in the visiting room. What was the point of celebrating a birthday?

I thought. What meaning does celebrating the day you were born – the basis for so many joyous traditions – have when you live in a place empty of every trace of humanity?

I'd decided to let myself die. The idea had been stirring in me for a long time; my sentence only encouraged me. That was when a series of events plunged me into a state of fear and hope, at the same time.

It was 23rd December, the night before my mother and sister were due to visit. We'd already had dinner and done our homework. In preparation for their arrival, I washed my hair in the sink in our cell. I wanted to look good, even if I was skinnier; strong, even if tired; brave, even if despondent. I was lying on my straw mattress, hair wet, mind wandering, when all of a sudden, the door opened – which never happened at that time of night. A guard entered and ordered me to come with him. A voice crackled in the outdated intercom. A few girls sat up in their bunks. The guard listened to the orders in Mandarin, annoyed to see me stock still, hair damp, a dumb look on my face, in no hurry to heed his instructions when he obviously wanted to get this over with so he could go back to sleep. 'Where are you taking me?' I asked. 'Gather your things. Let's go. You'll be back in a few days.' I had no things, or so few that when a girl held out a jacket, I took it, and followed him.

✳✳✳

Outside, the polar cold stung my skin. We began running through the snow, our breath making small white clouds in the dark. Then we reached the building where I'd been tried in November. We were kept waiting at the door for a few, endless minutes. One man spoke into his walkie-talkie and, infuriated at being the plaything of the warders' obscure orders, I interrupted the guard who was announcing our arrival: 'I don't know where you're taking me, but I've got visitors tomorrow. It's my birthday. My mother and my sister are coming. They're already in town. You can take me wherever you want, but after they come. Please, let me see them first. The voice from the walkie-talkie stopped for a moment in surprise. Then he growled something, I didn't catch what. 'That's a no,' said the guard. More men showed up. I was cuffed hand and ankle. I froze at the awful sensation of metal on my skin; another hand yanked a hood over my head. As before, chains and total darkness meant I was being transferred somewhere. I heard the engine of a car getting closer, hands sliding open a door. As I sat down on the seat, the acrid stench of the heating filled my nostrils.

We drove through the night. Right then, they could've marched me out and shot me down in the middle of the snowy desert. I wouldn't have felt a thing. The energy they'd lavished on killing me slowly had been in vain. I was dead inside already.

They took me to another jail. Not the one where I'd been locked up in 2017, but a bigger one with more violent police. While a pair of hands filled my own with a prisoner's necessities, which I knew all too well (toothbrush, black slippers, khaki hose, orange jumpsuit), others roughly shoved clippers through my unruly mane. Uneven thatches of black hair tumbled onto my shoulders.

'Is all this really necessary?'

'Keep asking questions, and we'll shave it all off,' replied one of the two guards, a man. The other, a woman, took a step back to appraise the carnage. 'Why, you look so pretty! You really, really do!' she joked. Everyone laughed, as if she'd made a wisecrack, a bit of schoolboy humour, and I was just being too sensitive for their good-natured ridicule; I was making too big a deal over a little bit of hair.

'What is that thing?' the female guard asked, taken aback. She pointed at the electronic bracelet on my arm. I'd completely forgotten it even existed. 'Let's take that off,' said another guard. After several tries, they gave up. That insufferable bracelet just wouldn't come off, as if the camp were keeping tabs on me forever. 'We'll take you back to the school to get it off,' the female guard declared. My stomach knotted up just then. What did she mean, go back to the camp? If I went back there, I'd never get out again. That much was certain.

'No, I'll take it off myself!' I tore at the tiny thing with all my strength, digging my nails into my skin, making red marks. I thought about the other option: going back to the camp to get it off. I pulled even harder, grimacing. Finally, the bracelet slipped over my fingers. Relieved, I held it out to the female guard.

I rediscovered the cold, stifling air in a cell where 30 women breathed, slept, ate, and wept all huddled together, packed in like sardines. In this familiar décor that reawakened my early trauma over detention, I made out, to my great surprise, a face I knew. Almira.

Almira was 55 years old, a tall four-square woman, one of those people whose contagious joy warms you when she talks to you. When she came towards me, I was stunned. They'd shaved her head too, and she'd lost a lot of weight, as if her belly and arms had been stripped of their flesh. Her whole body reeled and tottered, her legs threatening to give way any minute. She was happy to see me, couldn't get over our reunion after all these years, and in this miserable hole. 'Gulbahar! Gulbahar, is it really you? How are you? Weren't you in France? What are you doing here? Did they take Kerim, too?'

Almira had been Gulhumar's middle school literature teacher in Karamay. Last October, people from the Central Commission for Discipline Inspection had come to interrogate her. According to them, a fight had broken out at school between Han and Uyghur students. Almira replied that she'd never heard of such a fight. That was when they'd hauled her off to the police station. During questioning, the police accused her of favouring instruction in Uyghur and not Mandarin. She was confused: hadn't she been brought to the station to talk about a fight between students? Evidently not. The police were interested in her job, the content of her lessons, her political opinions, and her religious beliefs. She protested, saying she just taught literature, but in vain. Around her, the police were shouting, saying she promoted separatism in her classes. Then they began to beat her. A doctor attended her daily beatings, and whenever she would faint away from 'one too many blows,' the police would take a step back and the doctor would intervene to see to her wounds. Then the beatings would resume. Almira never confessed a thing for she had nothing to confess. And yet after two weeks, they transferred her here. That had been three months ago.

I brooded over poor Almira's story. Then I ran into Zahida, another old friend from Karamay. Another face from the past disfigured by detention. She was sleeping a few bunks away from me and, after a few days spent pacing the cell, she finally told me what they'd done to her. That was when I realised that the police officers, their minds dulled from all that brainwashing, had no mercy at all for us. They would drag us through repression and into madness, through an unchecked bloodbath if they had to.

When we lived in Karamay, Zahida's son Dolkun had been in Gulhumar's class. She liked the boy, a quiet, reassuring presence, always in a good mood and ready to please. When we left, we lost touch with them. Dolkun looked a lot like his mother. Maybe I thought so because I'd never known her as anything but a widow. Zahida's husband had died very young. His death had not only left them inconsolable but led to a series of financial issues that we – friends from school and the neighbourhood, tried to ease. But though Zahida struggled to raise her two children on a single income, she never complained. She was short, thin, a tiny woman with boundless kindness and courage.

She never even mentioned the reason why, one morning in May 2017, the police knocked at her door and took her in. They didn't need a reason. They'd make something up once when they were reading her file, safe behind the precinct walls. So when Zahida went with them, she hadn't suspected a thing. No doubt she'd thought she'd be back from the station by nightfall, after several hours of questioning spent gulping down gallons of tea. But this time, the police wanted her to sign a confession. They shook the paper under her nose, putting the pen back in her hand when she let go of it, weary of protesting that she'd done nothing. That this was just a big misunderstanding. Zahida was stubborn.

They were too. They locked her up in jail. They came back every day, insistent, paper in hand. She refused to sign. I don't know how long all that went on, but one morning, in the interrogation room where she was explaining for the nth time that she was innocent, she heard screams. Muffled, at first. As she pricked up her ears, listening more intently, they grew louder. They were torturing someone next door. What could they be doing, to make someone scream like that? The pain had to be unimaginable. It had to stop. 'Stop! Stop!' she cried out to the men who stared back at her, unblinking. That was when she recognised the voice. It was Dolkun, her son. They were torturing her son, and on the table before her, the confession awaited her signature. Zahida signed, trembling. She did as she was told, and gradually, the screams stopped. Then she was sentenced to 15 years in prison. Since then, she'd been in jail, waiting for her transfer. That had been two years ago. She never found out what had happened to Dolkun: if he'd died in the room next door, or if he'd been sentenced and sent to prison, too.

And me? What had happened to me in the last two years? Could my suffering be compared with Almira's? Zahida's? No, I couldn't make that comparison. Yes, I'd been mistreated. Abused. The warders, police officers, and teachers had used coercion techniques, every possible threat to make me confess to trumped-up crimes. But apart from a few slaps and punishments, I had never been beaten like Almira. My child had never been tortured as those brutes had Zahida's. Yes, I'd been a victim of the same vast 're-education' project as they were, but I belonged to a class of special detainees: those who'd lived in exile. Either that would work in my favour and help get me out of this nightmare (my family working from France to negotiate my release), or else it would send me tumbling into abysses even deeper still, where some terrible fate had been reserved for me. In the eyes of Chinese authorities, I'd committed an irrevocable crime by leaving Xinjiang for France. I'd been sentenced to seven years of 're-education,' then yanked out of camp after a few weeks. That wasn't a good sign.

Almira and Zahida were Uyghurs, like millions of others living in Xinjiang. I, however, was the wife of a French political asylee, a Uyghur living in exile who'd been naturalised: in short, a French citizen. If I ever got out of this awful place, they couldn't keep me in Xinjiang forever. Kerim had told me that time and again. Rather than making me appreciate my position, the fates of my friends only saddened me all the more, as their future, whether in prison, a camp, or in Xinjiang, seemed equally dark. Even now, I didn't dare think of Zahida. The very thought of her sent me hurtling into dizzying anguish. She was sentenced to 15 years! 15! And Almira, what could she hope for? After six or even ten months in jail, she'd probably face a sentence of several years in a 'school' where propaganda would triumph over her memories, her soul, her faith. In the worst case scenario, she too might end up in a prison where they would rob her of her dignity. No matter what happened, Almira wouldn't get out for ages, not until her hair was grey and her face lined, her body withered away to a boniness that was not the result of age but mistreatment. She would go back to her apartment in Karamay, but would anyone be waiting? Her husband? Her son? Before then, they too would be imprisoned for some made-up reason. My husband and daughters were safe. They could never be taken from me.

Almira would resume a life that was by all appearances quiet but in reality hellish, for never, not even once she'd paid for her 'crimes,' would the police leave her alone. They would show up at her door unannounced, and she'd have to answer their intrusive questions, feign insufferable obedience, demonstrate her faith in the Party, maybe even denounce her neighbours or Uyghur acquaintances to buy herself a short-lived peace. Almira would be living in one prison or another for the rest of her life. Just like my mother, my brothers, my sisters, and their children. Like all Uyghurs.

A few weeks later, I ran into yet another person I knew: another woman, also a Uyghur. We'd met at the other jail back in 2017. We hadn't been on the same side of the bars, so to speak, since she used to run the jail in question. Like many Uyghurs who'd opted to save their skins by joining the police or going into civil service, she was sympathetic to detainees. I don't really know why, but this woman grew fond of me, and when I met her again in this jail, she gave me a big smile and asked what I was doing here, her voice tinged with enthusiasm, as if she had run into me on a street corner. After listening to my tale, she promised to find out more about my case. A few days later, I ran into her again, and she confirmed my theory: in early 2018, detainees who had lived abroad were being set aside for a special fate. Little by little, authorities were transferring them from camps to jail. A woman whose daughter lived in Holland had left the same camp I had half an hour after my departure. A few days later, another woman showed up here. Her brother was living in the United Kingdom. They'd both been put in cells next to mine.

After that, I kept going back to the calculations in my head. The more I thought about it, the more obvious it seemed: we Uyghurs tied to foreign countries by an invisible thread – a daughter, a son, a cousin, an aunt, or in my case, an entire family – were a real conundrum to the authorities in Xinjiang. On one hand, they had reserved maximum sentences for us. For in their paranoid eyes, we were unforgivable traitors. We were spies in the pay of the West. On the other hand, our loved ones in Europe had to come out and agitate for our release – that much was clear. Discrimination against us had outraged Kerim for years. I had a hard time picturing him lounging on the sofa, waiting for me to return. Gulnigar was still young, but Gulhumar, with her boundless endurance, was probably not sitting around twiddling her thumbs either. They'd had more than enough time to notify the French authorities. The Chinese had to justify the reasons for my imprisonment. But they had nothing on me. They were stalling for time. The proof? The judge's administrative dithering over our household registration and the sale of the apartment in Karamay: they were looking for an excuse to hold onto me. To justify my 're-education.' So there was hope after all. I had to hang on. If they had nothing on me, and the French authorities were negotiating for my release, China would be forced to withdraw. There was hope.

18. Battles With Tasqin

11th March 2019

The interrogations were like a game of chess. Both players – policeman on one side, detainee on the other – had their pawns, their bishops, their rooks, their queen, and their king. One player's pieces advanced across the board according to a strategy that was always changing in response to the other player's moves. Admittedly, the policeman always came in with an upper hand that would allow him to win the game, or so he thought. But as the interrogations piled up, prisoners on the far side of the table became better able to anticipate their opponent's moves. They learned the tricks, the secrets, dodging traps the other had laid. I'm not saying that I excelled at this game, but I had picked up techniques from policemen trying to get you to talk by provoking a combination of anger, fear, and despair. They'd show you a photo, the face of a loved one, or else a series of text messages to throw you off-balance. You had to remain utterly in control of your emotions. The slightest shudder was like cracking open a door that they'd kick in with their boots. A veteran now of several hundreds of hours of questioning, during which I'd racked up major defeats and then, over time, small victories, I wasn't too worried when the police had summoned me a week earlier. It was just the same old prison routine. I did what I was told with the unthinking obedience of prisoners who are worn down from complying and save their strength for use on special occasions – that is to say, when they smell death. Interrogations? I'd been through dozens of them. One more wasn't about to send me to the grave.

The man waiting for me in the interrogation room didn't look like any officer I'd seen before. He didn't behave like those who, soon exasperated with the laborious slowness of interrogation, wound up screaming threats or insults. No, this man, of Kazakh descent, displayed an unsettling placidity. His icy courtesy indicated that he handled important cases. This was no underling, but a chief of domestic intelligence. His name was Tasqin.

He looked me right in the eye, his hands on the thick red folder that held my file.

'Gulbahar Haitiwaji, I have been hearing about your case for two years. I have decided to see to it personally. I went to Ghulja to see your family, and to the university in Ürümqi to meet your teachers. I wish to close this case. We must be done with it.'

'We will begin by reviewing everything, from the beginning,' he went on with perfect calm as two policemen cuffed my wrists and ankles. I didn't understand and, faced with my questioning air, he explained. 'We will look at your case from the beginning, which is to say, 1985.' My heart skipped a beat. My body trembling on one side of the chessboard, I realised that I was facing a worthy adversary, against whom my tactics of evasion might not work.

In 1985, Tiananmen hadn't happened yet, but China's universities were already incubating the seeds of a desire for change on the part of students. In Ürümqi, the students – a mix of minorities – demanded reforms, sweeping aside questions of ethnicity and economics alike, prefiguring demands that would be shouted and blazoned on signs by the students in Beijing who occupied the square in front of the Forbidden City in the spring of 1989. The month was December, windy and austere. That winter had seen a lot of snow, and among the crowd of young men and women gathering in the city's main square, bundled up and bursting with hope, were Kerim, our friends, and myself. Of those moments together, I remember a festive atmosphere, simple joys. We had few resources at our disposal, but we approached discussions about the future with a carefree enthusiasm that fuelled hope for the change an entire generation of young people longed to see happen, one way or another, in the society where they were building a life for themselves.

With a certain naïveté, we thought that the government would heed our peaceful demonstrations and that, little by little, the change for which we all so devoutly wished might come, if not for us, then at least for our children. The movement was repressed, not by force as at Tiananmen, but by a 're-education' already up and running at universities. After that December, bureaucrats came to tell us time and again what we had done wrong. We didn't realise back then that the authorities were brainwashing us. Once we moved to Karamay, we forgot the incident. That is what I remembered. That is what I told Tasqin, my heart pounding. He studied me with his stern gaze, searching for a flaw in my story, so he could lay a trap for me. But he found none.

The conversation then drifted to my life in France, our arrival there, my job in a noisy cafeteria in one of the office skyscrapers within the keep of La Défense, my social circle (diaspora families), my hobbies (cooking, yoga). Nothing I hadn't already detailed to the police millions of times.

At the end of the day, after ten hours of interrogation, I was allowed to return to my cell. Then things took a strange turn. Early the next morning, at the same time, Tasqin summoned me again. Believe me when I say that in Chinese jails and 're-education' camps, no one is ever interrogated two days in a row. You're thinking of ending your days in this rathole when suddenly a police officer summons you. He tells you he's been to visit your family, that they've been going over your case file at the station, and that, yes, there's been some progress, but you won't be allowed to leave, of course, until you're fully reformed. In short, he makes you believe that you'll soon be released. This way, prisoners don't completely lose hope. Instead, they cling to every crumb of information tossed their way. This is their nourishment in the long months after every interrogation, since they've been told they'll be freed if they're patient. So they show how patient they can be. They grit their teeth a little harder. But getting summoned two days in a row? I assure you, it never happens.

In the cell, the girls were swarming around me like bees.

Advice and opinions whizzed by. I couldn't figure out whether this second summons augured well or ill. For the girls, one thing was certain: if Tasqin wanted to see me again, that meant my case was entering its final phase. I'd soon find out what fate the Karamay police had in store for me. The thought excited and terrified me in equal measure. On 5th March at 9am, we started the interrogation in the same way, with the 1985 demonstrations: what friends were there, what political opinions I entertained at the time, what student groups I was a part of. Every single question he asked was the same as from the day before. Then the conversation turned once again to our arrival with Kerim and the girls in France, my job in a cafeteria, my social circle, my hobbies. After ten hours, I went back to my cell, my throat dry, my body tingling all over. The next day, Tasqin summoned me yet again.

The interrogations went on for six days. As he watched my exhaustion grow from going over my life from every angle, he gained ground. He punctuated my account with subtle touches, remarks meant to lead me to self-criticism. 'You do know that the organisation your husband's in belongs to Rebiya Kadeer? You do know she's a terrorist?' For five days in a row, I told him, 'No, neither my husband nor Rebiya Kadeer are terrorists, and that 'the France Uyghur Association he's a member of does not disseminate separatism but Uyghur culture.' I, too, was stubborn, but after each of my 'wrong answers,' he would merely reassert, 'Rebiya Kadeer is a terrorist.'

'No, I'm telling you she isn't.'

'Rebiya Kadeer is a terrorist. Repeat after me. You don't seem be taking the easy way. Must we resort to the hard way?'

On the sixth day, I gave in. Not because I believed the pack of lies he was forcing down my throat, but because I wanted him to shut up. I wanted the nightmarish interrogations to end. Over and over and over again, he made me say what he wanted to hear, and when he'd had enough, he said: 'That's enough. You're ready.' The 'Queen of Interrogations' – that was his ironic nickname for me. I blame myself for everything now.

Yesterday, 10th March, there was no interrogation. The police came for me. Just like every other time, they shackled, cuffed and hooded me. Tasqin joined us outside. As we navigated a series of corridors and stairways, I steeled myself for torture. I'd said goodbye to my fellow detainees with a sad look in my eye. I just had the feeling I was never going to see them again. Almira returned my weak smile. I thought about the beatings she'd received. How did it feel, being tortured? What techniques did the police use? Would they strike me with their fists, as they had Almira? Torture one of my sisters, as they'd tortured Zahida through her son? I hoped they'd hit my head but not my body; there was no body left. I was a bag of skin and bones now.

These were the thoughts that occurred to me as we made our way through the soulless corridors of the police station. Then the policemen ushered me into a room where a rotund little man and a group of women were waiting. His name was Luo, 'Chief Luo.' When he saw me, he started yelling, 'What's with these shackles and these cuffs? Take that hood off!' Embarrassed, the officers rushed to obey.

We headed upstairs in silence. They pushed me into a room. I scanned the space for torture devices, chains, ropes – anything that might confirm the bad feeling gnawing away at me. But all I could see were a small table against the wall, under a big mirror, and an adjoining closet with two sinks. This was no torture chamber. It was... a bathroom.

I'd been wearing the same jumpsuit for months. It was soaked in sweat and the humiliations I'd had to endure. It reeked of the filth of imprisonment. The stains and rust attested to the shameful state I'd been left in. Now, all of a sudden, I was being dolled up like an actress before a show.

A handful of women bustled about me, tugging on my short, limp locks to dye them with a brushstroke, tossing my prisoner's duds into a corner of the room, buzzing around my face with mascara, lipstick, and eyeshadow from a drawer of the table. One of them was applying eyeliner to my swollen eyelids, another dabbing at my hollow cheeks with blush. I had no idea why, but these policewomen were busy making me look like a human being again.

'Apparently, you were very cooperative during your interrogation. You're going to say everything you said to the agent all over again, but this time, for the camera. Are you on board?' Chief Luo asked me, as if all this fuss – makeup artists, brushes, mascara, lipstick – were a perfectly normal part of my day. 'In exchange, we will improve your living conditions.' We went back downstairs and into a cold, empty room with tinted windows. A camera presided from a tripod.

The women in jail had told me about police techniques for filming your confession. Once they had it on tape, they could dangle your own words over your head at any time, as blackmail.

To make you cooperate with the police or, on the contrary, to keep you quiet about the abuses you'd suffered. If you spoke up, the video would be spread online, and people would see you, all dolled up and decked out, talking about how you'd slandered the Party then asked its forgiveness. That way, no one would believe you when you protested your innocence. The Party would always have a hold over those it was monitoring.

Blinded by a wall of lights, disoriented, I heard someone shout, 'We're rolling!' I launched into the statement I had in my head, which Tasqin had made me rehearse a few minutes earlier. Not a word of it was true. It was all lies. At the time, I had no choice. It was too late. I'd already confessed my 'crimes' to the agent at the jail and, caught up in the hellish cycle of confessions, I was too afraid of the reprisals that backpedalling might bring.

'My name is Gulbahar Haitiwaji.'

Luo's face was deep in shadow, but I made out his encouraging smile. He bade me continue my soliloquy with a wave of his hand. I obeyed.

'I was born in Ghulja, in Xinjiang province, in China, on 24th December 1966. I lived in Ghulja till the end of middle school, and then, in 1984, I left to study at the Petroleum Engineering School at Xinjiang University in Ürümqi, where I had been offered tuition, housing, and meals. But these privileges were not enough. I was a discontent. That is why I took part in the demonstrations in December 1985. I regret my acts and beg forgiveness. In 1988, I was transferred to Karamay. In 1990, I married Kerim Haitiwaji, and our daughters were born in 1992 and 1997. In 2002, despite a comfortable lifestyle, my husband went to live in Paris, France.

I tried to stop him, but he didn't listen. He took a wrong turn when he became involved with the France Uyghur Association. My daughter, Gulhumar Haitiwaji, followed her father and was led astray. This is a completely illegal organisation, under the control of Rebiya Kadeer, that advocates independence and separatism. Rebiya Kadeer is a liar and a terrorist. Do not join her organisation. If you are already a member, quit now. Kerim, Gulhumar, I'm begging you, quit that organisation and do not do anything bad to China. Each time I visit my family in Xinjiang, I see the progress China has brought to our province. No matter what happens, I will choose China. I am on its side. I hope you will make the same choice.'

Afterwards I wept, alone in a cell. I had been living in hopes of being freed, and now that I'd been promised a better future, I was wracked with guilt. China had stolen my very thoughts from me. In one video, Rebiya Kadeer had said that one day China would force the Uyghurs it was imprisoning to criticise her in short videos, and that Uyghurs living abroad must never believe the words of those who, under duress and threat of violence, had collaborated with the Chinese police. But even if everything I'd said was but a pack of lies, would I be able to look my loved ones in the eye when I told them I'd had no choice? Kerim, Gulhumar... would they ever forgive me for denouncing them? I felt like I'd betrayed them, dishonoured Rebiya Kadeer, and nothing and no one could change any of that now. Was it not better to die head held high, mind and heart free even if my body was in prison, than to escape on my knees, my head filled with filth and lies, humiliated by the disappointed looks of those who beheld my weakness?

19. Freedom?

12th March 2019

I deliberately refused to respond. I barely glanced at Tasqin when he said, 'You're free.' He went on. 'Did you hear me? You should be happy. You're getting out of here.' Lying on my straw mattress, I turned my back to him. My eyes were wide open, staring at the wall blistered by damp. What was he waiting for? My thanks?

How many times had I pictured this moment for myself while lying in the dark, bereft of hope? I'd imagined the intense joy that would flood my being, and yet now, when I was being told that I'd be rejoining the world of the living at last, I felt empty, drained, stripped of the slightest human emotion. My mind was dark, not a single ray of light filtering in. An opaque mass of lessons, interrogations, abuse, bumping up against one another. They formed a shapeless pile of painful memories I couldn't look away from. That man had broken my body, my soul, and though the thought of seeing those I'd betrayed in my weakness terrified me, that arrogant man, one of the hundreds responsible for my suffering, had the gall to declare I was free! At that moment, I was overcome by a strange combination of pride, weariness, and fear. I was free. Or so I thought.

20. Fruit and Mint Tea

15th March 2019
Karamay

Waking to the smell of fresh bread tickling your nostrils. Sitting up on a soft mattress and pushing back the white sheets you'd been swathed in all night. Setting your feet down, head still heavy with sleep, on a crimson rug while taking in everything around you: the window, with its reassuring light, so alive, filtering through the slats of the electric shutters. The table, set with a basket of fruit, a carafe of water and clean glasses, juice, and a teapot that an expert hand will fill with fresh mint leaves and boiling water in just a few hours. The white walls with their simple decorations, finely wrought mirrors and a few frames.

This was my ritual every morning. I let my gaze sweep over the silent and immaculate room, which I never left except to go to the bathroom or take a shower. The first time I woke up here, I'd thought it was a dream. Then I soon realised it was the umpteenth nightmare. I wasn't free. I was living in a gilded cage, the building adjacent to the jail where I'd been held in 2017, the building where the police lived.

A group of eleven police officers – eight women and three men – took turns keeping watch over me day and night. When the house was steeped in the silent torpor of dawn, my jailers were still sprawled on the sofa and armchairs in the living room next door to my big bed. It was strange, seeing them like that – slouched and slumped in those disjointed poses that only sleep and death provide. Even the flatscreen TV was in sleep mode. I would turn it on later. I spent a lot of time in front of the TV. Not because I liked watching it so much, but because losing myself in cooking shows and catchy jingles helped me forget. In detention, there was nothing more terrible than the sound of silence: that damp, sticky silence where you could hear the prison creaking and draughts brush along the icy walls. Here, everything was warm, soft, no corners anywhere. If I felt a shiver down my spine, I turned up the volume on the TV.

Taking in one show after another also helped keep me from thinking. I still didn't know why I was here, if I was to be freed or if, on the contrary, they intended to keep me under surveillance for years. Who knew? I wouldn't have put it past them. At any rate, no one had seen fit to tell me anything, and I hadn't asked – for fear I'd be tossed back in a cell. But I found the cosy atmosphere equally comforting and worrisome. What Uyghur prisoner has ever been told: 'Your mission right now is just to eat, rest, and watch TV. You mustn't think about anything else.' The solicitude they showed, through cooked meals, new clothes, and cleaning products, gave me cause for concern, especially since what I glimpsed in their eyes wasn't compassion, but anxiety about following their superiors' orders to the letter. The first few days, I barely nibbled at the steaming Uyghur dishes they brought me. I'd eye the apples without touching them, as if they were poisoned. They'd insist I eat more than was reasonable. Gaining back the weight I'd lost in detention seemed to be a crucial stage in my recovery for them. 'Go on, eat up, have an apple,' one of the policewomen told me on the third day. We ended up sharing it.

The policewomen didn't watch over me so much as keep me under surveillance. The minute I moved to the open window to gaze at the tropical garden next to the house, they came over to me with worried looks. Whenever I luxuriated for a few too many minutes in the bathroom, they'd be tapping on the door: 'Gulbahar, are you all right in there? Is everything OK?' They were afraid I'd kill myself.

But I had no desire to die. I'd given up on the idea ever since the police told me I'd be allowed to call my family. Kerim, Gulhumar, Gulnigar.... I soon realised that, as ever, I would be afforded no privacy. Once again, I'd have to lie. Regurgitate the propaganda of the Communist Party, which resorted to the most twisted tactics to keep the fate of Uyghurs in China hidden. The police began making me rehearse my lines. I only remember the general thrust: 'I'm doing well, don't worry, I rented an apartment in Karamay. I'm alone. Don't worry.'

A date was set for the big day: early afternoon, 18th March. By then, Kerim would surely be home at the apartment and Gulhumar at work. Were the police trying to entrap him? How would Kerim and Gulhumar react when they heard my voice? Would they realise I was being forced to spout a pack of lies? Would the deafening silence all around me during the call tip them off that I wasn't alone, that I was on speakerphone surrounded by police officers busy scribbling my husband's and my daughter's words down in notebooks?

❀ ❀ ❀

Sunlight flooded the room now. Soon everyone would be up. I could hear birds cheeping outside, and the purr of car engines one street over. One of the policewomen muttered something. I watched as she curled up under her blanket and went back to sleep in a rustle of breathing. The women slumbering here did not have their faces harrowed by imprisonment. Their uniforms were spotless, filled out with healthy curves. Seven of them were Han, and the last Uyghur.

Among them was one named Wang Qian. I knew her from jail. She had stood out for her sadism there. She'd often come around to our cells and complain about the stomach aches she got from the meals in the other wing of the police station: they were just 'too rich.' She'd laugh and say, 'Guess I had too many meat kebabs!' Staring right at us as we sat on the floor, our stomachs growling from being filled with only broth thin as water. As coincidence would have it, here she was, my jailer again. But this time, she was the one sleeping on the floor.

I didn't blame that woman anymore. Even though she once made me suffer, I'd have gladly given her my bed. I no longer felt hatred for Wang Qian or her colleagues, for as I observed their faces – either impossibly young and pitted with acne, or else older, the faint wrinkles coming in – all I saw there were normal lives. Normal women, with normal lives. Lives with husbands, children, maybe fiancés. They were women just like me.

The Uyghur policewoman's name was Yultuz and, ever since I'd found out she was the same age as Gulhumar, 27, I'd been overcome with affection for her. Sometimes we went out for walks together in the garden. On one of these strolls, she shared a few snippets from her life – inconsequential anecdotes, always with her sparkling laughter. They did me good. Yultuz was engaged. I told her about my daughters, their childhood here, their studies in France: Gulhumar pursuing marketing, Gulnigar at business school. Yultuz looked at me starry-eyed. She could've been Gulhumar. She could've been my daughter. Except she'd thrown her lot in with the other side. She was a cop and I a 'terrorist.' And yet ethnically, we were the same. During our strolls, we whispered in Uyghur, switching swiftly to Mandarin at a disapproving glance from one of the Han policewomen. Yultuz celebrated Eid with her loved ones, and maybe not so long ago she once prayed without fear of being jailed, sent away, re-educated. Had she chosen to join the police so she wouldn't have to fear living in her own country? Was she aware that she was one of the regime's countless good little soldiers tasked with eradicating her own religion, her language, her traditions? Did Yultuz understand that China wanted to wipe Uyghurs off the face of the earth?

21. Phoning Home

2nd April 2019

I never got to ask her that question. Yultuz vanished. She was replaced with another policewoman, a Han. Our friendship had drawn the wrath of the bureaucrats watching our walks in the garden. I'd told her we shouldn't speak in Uyghur anymore, but we hadn't been careful enough. One of the policemen had notified his superiors, and then Yultuz had been reassigned to a different station. No one told me anything, but I knew. Not many people disappeared without a reason. Or at least that's what they'd have us believe, but when someone did disappear, that meant they were in trouble with the police. Even officers like Yultuz had reason to worry. Her orders had been to keep an eye on me, and her kindness towards me had resulted in her failing at her mission. It was my fault. I hope they didn't send her to be 're-educated.'

Still, for a few days now, I'd achieved a kind of balance – hanging onto a slender thread of happiness that might snap at any moment. The sun rose and set, and I didn't notice. The policemen spoke to me, but I didn't hear a word. My body was here, across from them, but my mind was already far away. The phone was all that mattered. Its tinkly ringtone. The few notes that rose into the air of the room, the same Unknown Caller that flashed on the screen. And my beating heart.

It began on 18th March. That day, the warm light that fell on the too-tidy hedges in the garden had a special glow to it. I wasn't strolling the dirt paths, trying to while away endless days where nothing ever happened. No, that day, I was pawing at the ground. That 18th March, I was wild. I wanted to shout out loud, to weep, to close my eyes to keep their words fresh: 'Gulbahar? Is that you?' 'Mom?' I lost my head that day. I heard the voices of Kerim and Gulhumar on the telephone.

The big day came before I had time to get ready. But how, you'll ask, do you even get ready for a telephone reunion with the people you love most in all the world, whom you've been kept from contacting for three years, whom you're not even sure are still hoping you'll come back? What do you say at a moment like that? Small talk, probably, because it makes you feel like everything's just the way it was before, that this call is to exchange the latest news from normal lives. That all of you are going back to work, or into the kitchen, and that at the end of the call, you'll sign off with 'Have a good day. See you tonight.' 'OK, see you.' Simple words have this much going for them: they help you channel your feelings. Joy, excitement, and other less rational emotions, the scars of detention, guilt over having vanished from the lives of my husband and daughters for almost three years, fear that they hate me for it, or hadn't fought for my release while I was rotting in a cell somewhere.

Yes, simple words were the right words. That's what I was telling myself that morning as the cool dawn was already giving way to tepid warmth and the policemen busied themselves with religious care to ready the table, the chairs, the mobile phone, the notebooks – in short, all the necessary paraphernalia for this call. I still wasn't sure what they were hoping to get from it. Information, naturally, but about what? It had been agreed upon that the two calls would take place in my room. The police had written questions down in the notebooks. They would make me ask them at the right time in the conversation, depending on how it went. A French-Chinese interpreter, a young man who'd spent eight years at a company in Marseille, would sit beside me. He would make sure I didn't pass on any personal messages or secret information. I didn't give a damn about secret information. The tension mounted in the room, but all I was thinking about were their voices.

When Kerim answered the phone, he was bustling around the foyer. I could hear sounds in the background, small items being moved around a hallway stand. He must've been looking for his keys. He was probably about to go down to the underground parking area to get his car and start his workday. Upon hearing my voice, he stopped short. That big, strapping, indomitable man was shaking like a leaf; I could feel it through the phone. 'Gulbahar, where are you? We've been looking everywhere.

We've been doing everything we can to free you,' he choked out. My heart was beating so hard in my chest that I couldn't make a sound. All around me, police officers were busy filling up their notebooks with Kerim's words. We didn't say much, just what mattered: I was alive and in good health. Kerim was well-versed in police interrogation techniques from Xinjiang. He knew I was surrounded by half a dozen Party henchmen. My silences answered all his questions. He didn't press me. Gulhumar didn't prove very talkative either. The policemen pointed that out to me after I hung up, suspicion in their eyes. In the background on her end, I could hear the intermittent whoosh of a vehicle moving at top speed. She was on a train. She didn't seem to care about hiding that fact. 'I'm going to a watchmaker's conference. For work, yes. It's in Switzerland,' was all she said after one of the policemen made me read the sentence in his notebook, his finger moving from word to word: 'Where are you right now? Are you alone?'

Kerim was still living in our apartment in Boulogne. Gulhumar was travelling for work. Gulnigar was doing well too, they said. I'd been absent for two years of their existence, and here they were, busy leading free and happy lives. When I hung up, a dark thought clouded the brief instant of feverish euphoria I'd been floating on weightlessly above the room, the police, their notebooks. If I ever got out of here one day and went back to my quiet life in Boulogne, I'd have to tell them about what had happened to me here in Xinjiang. It was all far too horrible to hear about, far too hard a story to tell. And yet I would have to.

How even to begin such a tale? How to tell them that I lived at the mercy of police violence, of Uyghurs like me who, because of the status their uniforms gave them, could do as they wished with our bodies and souls? Of men and women whose brains had been thoroughly washed, robots stripped of humanity zealously enforcing orders. Petty bureaucrats alienated by the hierarchy of a sprawling system in which those who do not denounce others are themselves denounced. Those who do not punish others are themselves punished. Persuaded we were enemies to be beaten down, traitors and terrorists, they took away our freedom. They locked us up like animals away from the rest of the world, away from time – in camps. There, those men and women brainwashed us. They propagated bad ideas, false ideas. They wanted to 'reeducate' us. They taught us to march in time to the national anthem in windowless classrooms where women collapsed from lack of oxygen only to be taken by guards even deeper into the bowels of a concentration camp system.

In the 'transformation-through-education' camps, life and death do not mean the same thing they do elsewhere. When the footfalls of guards woke us in the night, I thought a hundred times over that our time had come to be executed. When a hand viciously pushed clippers across my skull, and other hands snatched away the tufts of hair that fell on my shoulders, I shut my eyes, clouded with tears, thinking my end was near, that I was being readied for the scaffold, the electric chair, or drowning. Death lurked in every corner. When the nurses grabbed my arm to 'vaccinate' me, I thought they were poisoning me. Actually, they were sterilising us. That was when I understood the method of the camps, the strategy being implemented: not to kill us in cold blood, but to make us slowly disappear. So slowly that no one would notice.

We were ordered to deny who we were. To spit on our own traditions, our beliefs. To criticise our language. To insult our own people. I was made to believe that we, the Haitiwajis, were terrorists. I was so far away, so alone, so exhausted and alienated, that I almost ended up believing it. Kerim, Gulhumar, and Gulnigar: I denounced your 'crimes.' I begged forgiveness from the Communist Party for atrocities that neither you nor I committed. I regret everything I said. A hundred times over, I thought I was dead.

My thoughts were straying. I'd see things more clearly tomorrow. Maybe I wouldn't even remember any of this.

❁ ❁ ❁

Sometimes, I didn't know when or how all this began anymore. My memory failed me, my courage too. The next day, an extreme weariness would wash over me. I'd swing between contradictory moods, vague emotions that left me a few minutes after they'd come. My mind was nothing but a grey sponge now, worn from being squeezed out so often it couldn't hold onto the water of thoughts anymore. In the morning, I'd wake up drenched, my body shuddering in fits and starts, my mind filled with nightmares where frail shadows in jumpsuits still roam, short men shouting in Mandarin, Uyghur women begging their forgiveness. Monstrous camps. Kerim, Gulhumar, Gulnigar, will you believe me? If ever I have the courage to tell this dark tale someday, will you believe me? Maybe when they're around me, people will trade knowing glances. They'll say, those police interrogations from her trip to Xinjiang drove her off the deep end.

I did go insane in the camps, it's true. But everything that happened there was real. Nothing I went through was the manifestation of some morbid fantasy from a prisoner exaggerating her conditions. I was taken, like thousands of others, caught up in the mad whirlwind of China. A China that imprisons. A China that tortures. A China that kills its Uyghur citizens. One day, when I'm brave enough, I'll tell my story. So Kerim, Gulhumar, and Gulnigar will know. So the world will know.

22. Monitored All Day

6th April 2019

They've made it so I can't skip meals. If they see me picking at my food, they swarm around me, encouraging me to eat, as with a child who won't finish their plate. 'C'mon, Gulbahar. Have some more.' The fragrant dishes they bring me, the restorative sleep of nights spent curled up in a cosy bed, the yoga stretching on the thick rug in the room – all these finally overcome my mistrust. Little by little, I lower my guard. I gorge myself on the respite I've been offered. I don't hold back. Especially since everything here is subject to negotiation. Nothing's free. If I don't eat, I won't be allowed to call Kerim and Gulhumar (I've been permitted to call them once a day, sometimes once every other day). So I eat. I stretch. I sleep. Even if the faces of fellow prisoners left behind in the camps, and also the faces of my tormentors, still come back to haunt me. Even if I still jump at the slightest squeak of steps on linoleum, a distant slam of a door. For the serenity of my slumbering senses could be taken from me at any moment. I'm being allowed to believe I'll soon be free, but this prospect depends entirely on my cooperation with the police officers, whose goals I'm beginning to understand. If I resist, I'll be sent back to a camp. They've warned me of as much.

The calls were what tipped me off. For a few weeks, the frequency with which I was allowed to contact Kerim and Gulhumar astonished me. I'd call them each for a few minutes every day – to 'catch up,' as the police put it. Why did I, who had been sentenced to seven years of 're-education' and imprisoned for more than two, suddenly have a right to talk with my loved ones, deemed traitors living in exile in France? For what reason was I being made to live like this, in housing reserved for police officers, if not to be used as a bargaining chip, a tool in some negotiation?

Intelligence services in Xinjiang were interested in the activities of Kerim and Gulhumar. During the months I'd spent in jail, in one camp, in another, and then in jail again, my family had done their unrelenting best to figure out what had happened to me. They'd filled me in on all that over the phone: the fear that I was rotting away in a cell somewhere, the fear I'd been sent to a 're-education' camp or that my body had been tossed into a mass grave with other Uyghurs. How, for months, they reached out to everyone we'd known in Xinjiang: family, friends, acquaintances, and then how, after dead end upon dead end, false hopes and letdowns, a file with my name on it had found its way to the French Foreign Ministry.

I realised then that my hush-hush disappearance was no secret at all in France. Gulhumar was talking to reporters about me; she was demanding that China release me. On TV, she was openly condemning 're-education' camps. Kerim was sharing articles on his Facebook page. A petition was circulating online.

In the room, the officer across from me was scribbling something. He handed me his notebook, and I read his question aloud. Kerim or Gulhumar would answer. I'd hand back the notebook. This little routine would begin again. Around us, pencil-pushing policemen would transcribe these exchanges, the names and dates of media that Kerim and Gulhumar mentioned. Hunched over a computer, another officer would be checking news sites, Facebook profiles.

My room became the field headquarters for a Chinese intelligence operation directed against my own family, and I was part of it, my throat tight, unable to scream the truth into the handset. I had become a bargaining chip between my family and the police, the linchpin in ongoing siege warfare. I'd comply whenever a policeman gave me a signal. I'd read off his umpteenth question whenever he handed me his damned notebook. The others kept scribbling away. 'Are you sure you're alone, Mom?' Gulhumar would often ask me. And with a heavy heart, I would reply, 'Yes, I am alone.' Lies leave a terrible taste in your mouth.

The police suspected Gulhumar of trying to take part in a certain 'conference,' a meeting where experts would be discussing human rights in Xinjiang and where she intended to tell my story. I couldn't really grasp the significance of this meeting, nor the repercussions it might have on the 'schools' in Xinjiang, but it was a huge thorn in the side of the police. They sought to sabotage it, and my role, once again, was to help them.

It was 20th March, the day of Nowruz. My call came through in the middle of a morning Gulhumar was spending with a handful of friends at Ikea. She picked up right away. In the background, I could hear a robotic female voice over the loudspeakers, children crying, the sound of shopping trolleys. Just another Saturday at Ikea. It was early in France. Gulhumar and her husband were probably going to have lunch with their friends afterwards to celebrate what was for Uyghurs the first day of the new year. The policeman handed me the notebook, and we were off.

'Where are you? In France? Don't go anywhere.'

'Yes, don't worry. We're not celebrating Nowruz with the community this year. I won't go. We'll be staying at home.'

'I'm not talking about Nowruz, Gulhumar. I'm talking about a conference abroad.'

Silence on the line. Gulhumar had moved away from her little group. Suddenly, I could hear her voice more clearly. 'I was supposed to go to Geneva for the annual session of the Human Rights Council. They invited me. But don't worry, I turned them down right after the first time you called. I'm surprised Chinese intelligence doesn't know that already.'

All around me, the police were staring daggers. They were about to explode. The tension racheted up in the room. Gulhumar was mocking them. Another officer handed me his notebook. I read off the words tonelessly: 'Gulhumar, this is very serious. If you have done illegal things, stop. If you have not yet done so, do not start. Be smart. Remove all the posts about what happened to me from your Facebook page. Do not speak about the Uyghurs and criticise the Chinese government in the media anymore. This is very serious. If you ever want to see me, you must take it all down.'

Wouldn't that make anyone crazy? Being jerked around like a puppet, a lure, used to blackmail my own family? Here I was threatening them, while in France Gulhumar and Kerim were doing their damnedest to free me by any means necessary. But so long as they continued to talk, I would not be released.

Gulhumar and Kerim had to be quiet and let my case fall off the radar of the French media and authorities. Then and only then would I be sent discreetly back to France. Once again, this logic underlined the sheer perversity of Chinese diplomacy. The authorities in Xinjiang were ready to sacrifice my camp sentence to stave off international criticism of their great 're-education' project. And of course, they were seizing this chance to make all the evidence of my detention in Xinjiang disappear. They'd already covered their tracks with my confession video, which they could use against me if I ever felt like going public once I'd been freed. Now they were trying to tie up loose ends with Kerim and Gulhumar by urging them to take down every piece of information – the articles, the petition, the testimonies – that bore witness to both the existence of the Xinjiang camps and my detention in one of them.

Right after the call, Kerim and Gulhumar began taking down their publications. The policemen had made a list of articles to be deleted and, in every call after that, we took stock of the 'great clean-up.' The Chinese police strategy was working: my story, which had dominated Uyghur diaspora discussion boards and social networks, was disappearing piece by piece. And here I was, still trapped, making sure over the phone that it happened. Oh, they were so clever.

One morning, when a policeman came to tell me my daily call would begin in a few minutes, I blew up. My eyes full of tears, I screamed: Enough. I won't play your warped little game anymore. They could just send me right back to camp, I didn't care. I didn't give a damn. I just wanted to stop lying to Kerim and Gulhumar. 'I want to stop lying to myself!' I kept crying; I couldn't stop. My entire outraged body was shaking, my throat on fire. 'I'll never call my family again!' The policeman lost his temper. He, too, was screaming in Mandarin. With all the yelling, other policemen came running, filling the hallway beyond the half-open door. The first one levelled an accusatory finger at me: 'Did we do all this for nothing, then? Don't make us regret it! What am I supposed to tell my superior if you don't make your call?' I was weeping; all those saved-up tears I hadn't cried before were coming out. But I held my ground. The police did not come back to my room with the phone that day. I turned on the TV, my eyes red, and sank into the couch, brooding on the prospect of a return to the camp – which I would not survive. That much was certain.

The policeman came back that night. He apologised, bringing up higgledy-piggledy the pressure he was getting from his bosses, the workload at the station, his wife, his children. I didn't know what to say. Now that the day was done and my rage had blown over, I was forced to admit that their offer of cooperation was still my only option. I was at an impasse. 'Don't worry. I forgive you,' I told him. He left, relieved to be able to inform his superiors that his mission – using me to silence criticism of the camps in the West – was back on track again. He left me alone the next day. The day after that, the calls started up again, and with them, the lies, the blackmail, and the threats.

23. Back in Karamay

12th April 2019

We were bouncing around in the back of a car on a clogged thoroughfare. I let my thoughts drift as I took in all of Karamay's sights. To either side of me on the worn seat sat a policewoman. This was my first outing. What a joy it was to see the city again, just as I remembered it; to note that restaurants and businesses hadn't been driven out. This Uyghur shop had everything you needed to make *laghman*, those long noodles you tossed with minced lamb, onions, eggplants, tomatoes, and peppers. And that one over there had wonderful fruits and vegetables. And ooh, the stall that sold meat skewers! We used to go there all the time for lunch with friends. The chunks of lamb were rubbed with salt, pepper, and cumin before being grilled. Once they were a nice golden-brown, they let off a delicious smell that filled the streets and brought passersby flocking. On the sidewalks, Han couples walked with a hurried step; Uyghur families waited by the entrance to a school; others chatted outside squat apartment buildings separated from one another by thick vegetation. Karamay had always had a lot of green space: parks, private gardens, rows of trees that grew longer every year as the city planted more along the canal. No doubt that was why the city, which like most northern cities looked barely Uyghur, nevertheless kept a certain charm.

We northerners believed southerly Kashgar to be the most Uyghur city in Xinjiang. The ancestral oasis town, located at the foot of the Tian Shan mountains that form a natural border between Kyrgyzstan and Tajikistan, was once a quintessential stop for merchants making their way along the Silk Road. They would halt their caravans in the shade of the esplanade of the great mosque. After days spent crossing the Taklamakan Desert, they would find, beneath its vast portico ringed with Arabian-style columns, a well-deserved respite. The Han-dominated north is always contrasted with the more separatist, more traditional south. And so, just as the capital city of Ürümqi radiates Chinese influence on nearby cities, for centuries Kashgar has been the shining light of Uyghur culture in southern Xinjiang.

We had stopped at a red light. Parents, children, and the elderly crossed the road in a procession. In the north, they also said that Uyghurs from Kashgar and its surrounding area practised a more devout, more doctrinarian form of Islam than in the north. Were you to visit that city, where Uyghurs are in the majority and Hans a minority – the opposite of Karamay – you would see that women took care to cover their heads in hijabs, and men let their beards grow. At any rate, that was how it still was a few years ago, before the decrees forbidding any outward display of Islamic beliefs complicated things.

Through the tinted window I glimpsed men with closely shaven heads, women with mops of hair coppery from highlights. Almost all of them went without face coverings. At the time when we were living here, men with long beards were already a rare sight, much less women in hijabs. At most a colourful silk scarf, like those my mother used to tie beneath her chin when she left the house. My sisters and I had never worn a veil. Nor had my daughters.

But don't get me wrong: I'm not saying all women in the south wore veils, and all northern women walked about barefaced. Let's say instead that I saw in these tendencies religious and cultural specificities peculiar to our ethnicity and that these tendencies doubtless stemmed from the way we Uyghurs had roots in different parts of Xinjiang; the way our customs and traditions had been more or less subtly refined, absorbed, or influenced by the mass arrival of Hans post-Communism. There's a word for this. 'Sinicisation.' Be that as it may, it was said that northern Uyghurs observed a more toned-down Islam, while southern Uyghurs represented the traditional fringe of our ethnicity.

We in Karamay did not feel China's influence when it fell upon us. A city born of the oil industry, Karamay was always Chinese in that respect. The Chinese built it to be by their refineries so they could drill for the black gold that has enabled us, families of workers and engineers, to settle down and make our lives here, Uyghurs and Hans alike. So it was that we always lived under a

Chinese flag, though that never stopped us – not for a very long time, at least – from being Uyghurs. We never felt Sinicisation laid down like a law as it was in southern cities like Kashgar, which saw the gems of its Islamic architecture crushed by Chinese diggers. We were not assimilated through the violence of a master urban plan that just a few years ago pruned away Kashgar's ancestral wonders: the Great Bazaar, with its winding alleyways roofed in corrugated tin, and the earthen-walled houses of the Old Town.

We were now going at a good clip, Karamay's apartment towers flashing by the windows. They looked the same as those in any medium-sized Chinese city. They were foursquare, lined up in a row, fitted into replicas of a single rectangular neighbourhood model. They weren't an eyesore, but they were devoid of charm. Now I realised that in the Sinicisation of city and countryside, the first signs of the 're-education' aimed at us had lain dormant. When Kashgar had surrendered to its new city plan, the people who lived in the little earthen-walled houses had been told that these transformations were for their own good, that destroying a few warrens of narrow alleys to make way for brand-new apartment buildings, or shrinking the esplanade of a mosque to wedge in a mall in no way amounted to an attack on their ethnicity's culture or religion, but quite the opposite: it was a way to give them access to modern conveniences. Today, the square in front of the old mosque in Kashgar is filled with giant screens. Citizens go there to pray, surveilled by the camera's all-seeing eye. Families that have lived for generations in the same house were displaced into new dwellings and told they would later profit from selling them.

A similar process went on in the camps: we were re-educated 'for our own good,' because there was 'evil' inside us, we were incessantly told. In Karamay, Ürümqi, Kashgar – no matter the particularities of local culture, Sinicisation, far-reaching and indestructible, always worked the same way. It slithered silently along, from minor intrusions to major aggressions. That was how we got to where we are now: 're-education.'

The policeman at the wheel swore in Mandarin at the congested evening rush hour. We were stuck in the street. It was the time of day when school bells rang, unleashing a flood of uniformed children onto the sidewalks. All around us, workers on bikes wended their way home through gaps in the traffic. We were coming back from one of those typically Chinese malls – the kind of building that moved here along with the Hans and was supposed to make it easy for you to do one-stop shopping. True, it was very handy. I'd gone to this mall once with Kerim and Gulnigar, over summer break in 2012. I remember the air conditioning wheezing at full blast in the shops.

Seven years later, I imagined my return to a quieter world. Inside the mall's luxurious main shopping area, built with the fake marble the Chinese seemed to love, salesgirls called out to you to come into their boutiques. The canned voices of advertisements mingled with the sounds of Chinese hits or K-pop. The blinding fluorescent light came in pink, white, and blue, falling on the polished tiles like in a nightclub. But no, this was merely the empire of fashion, household appliances, and beauty products.

I was being allowed to purchase a few clothing essentials. I'd been given enough money to replace the sweater, trousers, and socks that a policewoman had issued to me when I first arrived, as they were now threadbare. I was also counting on finding a new pair of shoes. This simple errand made me deliriously happy: I was buying shoes! What joy, after all this time my feet had spent pickling in prison-standard black cloth slippers.

But deep down, I was tormented with worry: what would happen if I ran into someone I knew? The police had deliberately taken me to the mall during the workday, just before lunch hour, so I'd be less likely to run into friends from Karamay, which I feared more than anything else. How would they have reacted upon recognising me, with my pallor and my boyish hair and my repulsive prison jumpsuit? They'd probably have realised I wasn't free when they spotted the escort following me through the shopping centre. Then they'd have given me a look full of that distasteful combination of fear and pity. Maybe some wouldn't even have dared say hello, out of fear that the police would later hold it against me. They'd just have peeked out of the corner of their eyes, whispering 'Isn't that Gulbahar? Yes, it is! But look at how she's changed.... Whatever happened to her?' From now on, I was one of those pariahs the police had seized upon, and the thought of bringing trouble to those I cared for terrified me.

But at the same time... I dreamed of running into Aynur. From behind the car window, I scrutinised every passerby, my heart pounding. I looked at height, the helmet of dark hair, the bundled-up profile, trying to pick out my friend or my sister Madina. I'd have loved to run into her in that mall. She often came and spent a few days in Karamay. Maybe we'd have recognised each other from a distance. We'd have rushed into each other's arms as the police looked leniently on. She'd have filled me in on the latest about her children and her husband, who'd all stayed at home in Ürümqi. I'd have made all sorts of small talk, carefully skirting the reality of the situation. She'd have gazed at me indulgently, the way people do when they know you're lying, but telling you with your eyes that it's all right, it's not serious, you're right to lie because we're in Xinjiang and in Xinjiang, where the police can do anything, you have to lie to protect your loved ones. No one here would ever hold that against you.

We wandered the shopping centre for an hour, or maybe just 20 minutes, I couldn't tell anymore, I'd lost all notion of time. Janitors were vigorously mopping the gleaming tiles in the atrium of the mall as we ducked into one, two, three, four boutiques. As we went along, the fabrics, scents, lights, the sweet voices of the shopgirls lulled me into a cottony feeling of wellbeing, such that I even managed to forget we'd be going back to the police station in a few hours. Time went by, we'd wrapped up my purchases and now noticed a few customers slipping across the polished tiles. We had enough time left for lunch. We sat down at the table of a restaurant looking out on the shopping area. The policemen ordered an array of items. Shopping had worked up an appetite. Faces buried in our bowls, we were so busy slurping down our noodles we never really had a chance to talk. As I watched them, busily filling their bellies, it occurred to me that nothing this weird had happened to me in a very long time. Here I was, bags full of pretty clothes at my feet, sharing a meal with policemen in a shopping mall where I'd roamed carefree with my family seven years ago. We reached the car and headed back.

It wasn't far to the police station now. I recognised the streets as we got closer. An atmosphere of dejection had fallen over the car. This day had gone like a dream. The police had promised we could go back and shop again. Not right away, but in a little while, they'd said. In the gloom of the backseat, I watched as my new shoes – a simple pair of black leather ankle boots with a high wooden heel, also black – gleamed in the dark. I'd put them on right away. There were laces to tie, and the toe, rounded and pointing ever so slightly upward, gave them a very feminine look. Gulhumar would've found them stylish. I'd tell her about them tomorrow, on the phone.

24. Cooking for Secret Police

6th June 2019

Our phone calls, brief but frequent enough, gradually helped me rediscover my place as a mother after being absent from my daughters' lives for over two and a half years. Gulhumar was pregnant. Kerim had told me some time ago, and I'd called her right away. 'I'll be there when the baby's born, I promise,' I told her right in front of the policemen who always attended my calls. There was something wonderful about those words, tossed out like a provocation amid the traumatising chaos of my life. Just like the baby who would be born in September. Hope lay in the immutable cycle of life going on despite tragedy. It lay in defeating Chinese 're-education' camps which, despite their tenacity in trying to silence who I am – a Uyghur, a free woman – did not succeed in doing so. It lay in the happiness of letting myself believe that one day in the not-so-distant future, I would take my place again among my loved ones.

Satisfied that Kerim's and Gulhumar's publications had vanished from social networks, the police had decided to reward me for collaborating by granting me a little extra autonomy. I was transferred to an apartment in downtown Karamay. There I lived with eleven police officers who shared my room, meals, and strolls from March onwards. It was a functional apartment that seemed to have seen a long series of tenants of varying degrees of cleanliness who had left behind a battered chair, a stained mattress and a few lumpy cushions leaking stuffing. I was in no hurry to fix things up and yoke myself to a big cleaning job in my new 'home' – the first after so many years. For a few days now, I had been rediscovering, with special pleasure, the pleasant sensation of living in a space that was mine – in short, not total freedom (I was cooking for eleven people who were watching my every move) but in a place whose atmosphere tried to provide an exact replica thereof.

That year, Eid al-Fitr fell on the 4th, just after my transfer. The police and I spent it together. I didn't like the idea; I'd never spent Eid with anyone but my family. But once again, I had no choice in the matter. I gritted my teeth and played the policemen's game, feigning blameless obedience. I readied the space for this time of sharing, busy in every room to impart an illusory feel of festivity, kindness, and friendship. The police were delighted to see me filling the refrigerator with fresh vegetables and handsome-looking cuts of meat. For a whole day, the ambiance was honestly joyful. It was the first time in years. Tired but satisfied at seeing my guests sated, I almost forgot the fundamental hypocrisy of the situation.

If there was a quality friends and family at home knew me for, it was my hospitality. I liked to have a fridge full of fresh, carefully selected food. I liked bustling about the kitchen for hours, kneading dough for *laghman*, rolling it under my fingers, stretching it out a thousand and one ways, and then making it into a long sausage. To ensure that the lamb fell off the bone when you picked it up with chopsticks, you had to cook it on a low flame all morning in a big pot. Cooking called for patience and meticulousness, just like other household tasks. I always ensured strict cleanliness: I aired the house every morning, even in midwinter, washed the curtains and linens and ironed the shirts, trousers and bedsheets. Not a single wrinkle escaped my notice.

Before stuffing our heads with lessons, grotesque military parades, and nights spent on a bed of wood or cement, the first thing they did in detention was to take away our personalities. When we put on that filthy jumpsuit and black cloth slippers, each prisoner became just like all the others. From that moment on, we were referred to not by our names but by numbers. Our souls withered away. In 're-education' camp and prison alike, submission abolished our wants, our passions. We were forbidden from speaking or writing things, which once made us unique, just as we were from marking our personal effects or our food: we slept on the same beds, we swallowed the same vile food. Through a series of punctures, the system drained us of who we were. Then, after emptying our minds, teachers crammed them with propaganda's dark ideas. We repeated the same phrases glorifying the Party. By filling ourselves with this pap, we were 're-educating' ourselves just as diligently. We lost our identity. Our selves crumbled away, all at the same pace, and when it was over we resembled each other physically and emotionally: misshapen phantoms, passive, unfeeling, and empty. We weren't people anymore then. We might as well have been dead.

So when the day of Eid came, and I set out pairs of chopsticks, cups for tea, and serving dishes for meat in sauce on the living room coffee table, I realised as I cast one final glance at the immaculate room, that this apartment, this new home, had begun to restore the life I once had. And that I was, not without difficulty, becoming Gulbahar from before the camps again.

25. The Truth is Voiceless

22nd June 2019

In Xinjiang, the truth has no voice. Those who have been in the camps know this. After weeks or months in the belly of the beast, in Chinese jails or 're-education' camps, you cannot tell your story. You can't tell the people who, although free in name, actually live under the yoke of the police. They will be afraid, even if they love you. They will fear for their lives.

The camps hang over conversations without being named explicitly. When they come up in the course of an anecdote or a stray comment, no one ever asks any questions. You gulp. You go on, pretending you didn't hear a thing. In this way, they are able to remain a kind of ghost story. Something you whisper to yourself in snatches. Everyone knows the camps are real. Everyone has loved ones who were locked away in them. And yet no one talks about it. And if no one talks about it, then the camps aren't real.

And so we each sink deeper into a series of little lies, harmless omissions that protect us. Concealing the truth used to outrage me during my calls with Kerim and Gulhumar, but time taught me to see that unpleasantness as a mere detail. It was but a drop in the vast sea of other minor annoyances that made up my life in Karamay. When I lined them up all, I realised that instead of ending my ordeal, it was being drawn out.

And yet, conditional freedom brought me back to life. I was given money, allowed to run a few errands in the outside world and do as I saw fit with the apartment. One day, I bought make-up and then walked into a hairdresser's where a friendly woman armed with a pair of scissors made me look like a city-dweller again – like any other woman on the streets. These small things made a big difference. Unable to face going backwards from here to either a jail or a school, I adhered to police tactics, albeit not without apprehension. While they gave me a slightly longer leash every day, they also forced me to lie shamelessly to those I loved: my family in France, who knew nothing about my actual living conditions, and then, my family in Xinjiang.

When I managed to get a visit from my mother and my sisters Nedjma and Madina, it was agreed that we would not speak of what I had been through, nor of any mutual acquaintances who had been imprisoned in Ghulja, Karamay, and Ürümqi. The police didn't even need to tell me not to bring it up: like myself, my mother and sisters just knew. Madina would not mention the 39 days she'd spent in a cell. Nedjma would keep quiet about the wounds her son had suffered upon being released from a 'school,' his shattered body propped up by crutches. And I would turn a deaf ear to the voices whispering inside my head.

The undreamt-of joy of being back together again was enough to satisfy us. Despite the lies traded between cups of tea and the silences that veiled our sufferings. Nothing was normal in Xinjiang, so why revel in the horrors inflicted on us? I wound up convincing myself that here, lies or the silences that surrounded them were worth more than the truth. We talked about the weather. My happiness knew no bounds.

The police planned to leave the apartment while my visitors were here. For a reason that escapes me, they didn't want my mother and sisters to find out I was being watched. Maybe it was because my case was the subject of contentious negotiations among higher-ups. Maybe because at this thorny moment in my journey, my loved ones couldn't be allowed to find out that someday soon, tomorrow or in six months, I might be sent back to France. Maybe also because this kind of surveillance was not legal, was in violation of my 're-education' sentence. After all, here I was, walking down the street surrounded by plainclothes police when the judge had sentenced me to seven years in a camp. It was all very strange.

At any rate, hosting them all by myself suited me just fine. When I'd call Madina to invite her over, she'd cried out joyfully: 'I knew you were out! Some people saw you in Karamay and told me right away! So you really are free!' What was the point of telling her the truth – that I wasn't? Besides, what Uyghur can claim to be truly free in Xinjiang? I shared her enthusiasm. Not even knowing if we were being watched could take that away from me. This was our reunion.

In Xinjiang, where draconian surveillance orchestrates people's lives, each street has its own 'neighbourhood committee.' From these offices, often on the ground floor of an apartment tower, volunteers and civil servants guide citizens' administrative initiatives. They themselves are locals, which makes them a sympathetic ear to talk to candidly about health, retirement, or education. In reality, these people must report on all neighbourhood events to the police.

The neighbourhood committees record the name, age, and profession of each resident in each apartment. This information is stored in a file updated with details of their travel and visitors. That is why police officers often come knocking unannounced to offer you their services and at the same time to see if everyone you're living with is reflected in their files. Every resident must fill out a declaration for anyone they're hosting. According to the '3-6-9' rule, citizens have three hours to declare their visitors to the neighbourhood committee, which in turn has six hours to notify the local precinct, which must register that visitor's contact info in their files within nine hours. There are no exceptions. Everyone followed the '3-6-9' rule.

My mother, sisters, and I knew this law would apply to their visit. But it also stymied the desire of the police to keep the reunion low-profile. So they'd decided to bend the law by passing themselves off as part of the neighbourhood committee. 'Can they do that?' I wondered, before getting a hold of myself. 'Of course they can. They're the police. They can do anything they want.' This way, we wouldn't need to declare the visit. Israyil, the current team leader, would pick up my family from the airport in his own car. In plainclothes, he looked just like any other driver. Same thing on the way back. No one would know about my presence in the apartment or their visit. By just knocking on the door and peeking in, the fake 'neighbourhood committee' could make sure everything was going as planned. If my mother, Nedjma, or Madina answered, they'd never know those ordinary-looking men with their affable smiles were actually my jailers. They'd answer any questions without suspecting a thing, because they had no reason to think those men were anything other than what they appeared to be: just the neighbourhood committee, checking up on things. Certainly not police. Once again, their tactics stirred fear in me but I accepted their bargain. I was only too happy to see my family.

On my end, I had 24 hours to deal with the mattresses slumped at the back of the closets and disappear the dirty dishes cluttering the sink. My mother and sisters were to find the apartment spotless. Nothing to make them suspect that I was actually under house arrest. We were going to spend three days together, and as the hours until they came ticked by, I let myself be swept along by intense joy, feverish excitement, and abject terror. I bustled about the place to channel these emotions that kept flooding through me, emotions that my years in a camp had made me lose or at least forget my ability to control.

In the end, the lies caught up with me. I wandered through the empty rooms looking for Madina's laughter, my mother stretched out dozing on the sofa, or Nedjma, busy in a bedroom with the TV on as background noise. Everyone was gone now. There was no one left. An icy draught swept through the apartment, despite the warmth of the June twilight. Would I ever see them again? When?

Nedjma had been the first to come up with the idea. 'What if we stayed here the whole time?' she wondered aloud the day she came. It wasn't the most comfortable apartment, but did we really have to go out to celebrate? We were reunited at last, and my mother, aching from the trip, needed rest. Sitting in the fridge were several dishes I'd made. We could fill the kettle and make some tea. And there was so much to talk about. So right then and there, we all agreed. We'd all spend the next three days right here, on the living room couch.

Now I sat on that very same couch, watching through the window as day waned, overcome by tremendous weariness. A weariness as great as the joy I'd felt welcoming them to my gilded cage. I couldn't sleep. My mind was just full of too much noise, a torrent of thoughts pouring into my stomach, clenched with sadness. I could still hear my mother's sobs, the soothing voices of Nedjma and Madina trying to calm her. And my lies.

They had made themselves at home with the same ease that accompanies every visit, scattering their personal effects here and there, the toothbrushes on the bathroom shelf, slippers on the door mat, stoles in warm tones on the coat rack by the front door, long dresses in the wardrobes. The place was new to them, but the familiarity they displayed in settling in recalled to me the vacations we once took together. They knew all my hiding places off the bat: the cupboard where I kept the condiments, where I'd put the mint, where I piled the clean, folded towels.

Among Uyghurs, we never insult a guest by asking how long they intend to stay. It doesn't matter if it's your sister, your brother, a cousin, or a perfect stranger. Your home is theirs. No need to tell them the pantry will always be stocked, they'll always have a bed and fresh sheets. They can stay as long as they like; it is an honour to host them.

My mother, Nedjma, and Madina thus believed themselves welcome here for as long as they wanted. Like back in Karamay, Ürümqi, or Ghulja. But to my great dismay, this was not the case. I'd made a deal with the police for three days. Three little days to make up for the time that the camps and the police had stolen from me – a real race against time. 'You know, Gulbahar, they can't stay for too long,' Tasqin had solemnly warned me. I'd nodded in agreement, wondering all the while how I'd manage to deny them the unlimited hospitality that was customary among us. Little by little, this pushed me into a series of lies I couldn't wriggle out of anymore, upsetting my sisters and saddening my mother in the course of our conversations.

Lively discussions filled the days. Madina threw herself into making us all laugh. On her phone, Nedjma showed us pictures of a cousin who'd been on a TV show watched by millions in Beijing. From her purse, my mother pulled a series of recent photos of Kerim, Gulhumar, and Gulnigar. I kept scampering back and forth from the living room to the kitchen, where water for tea was always on the boil. I didn't want to miss even the tinest scrap of their stories. I'd missed them so much.

And yet, a shadow loomed over our placid reunion. My mother just didn't understand: why hadn't I called them as soon as I'd gotten out of 'school' last March and invited them over here, or gone to see them in Ghulja? Why had I waited so long? 'I've had a lot to do, you know. I had to find an apartment in Karamay – no easy task. For several months, I was sleeping in hotel rooms. I couldn't have you over if nothing was ready. I wanted everything to be perfect for you when you came,' I told her, without managing to conceal my distress over that lie. Nedjma and Madina exchanged a knowing glance. They'd figured out that I wasn't free to speak. At that very moment, the police were probably listening in to our conversations.

Unlike my sisters, my mother didn't know much about the camps. Her advanced age and perhaps a certain ignorance kept her at a distance from such profound unrest, even if, like everyone else, she was questioned by the police on a regular basis. Admittedly, she did come to see me at Baijiantan, but visiting areas are a distorting mirror that hides reality. There is no way for visitors to guess at what goes on deep within the bowels of the prison, in cells and classrooms. Warders are always careful to greet all visitors with courtesy, handing out cups of water, asking after the health of visitors and their family. Sometimes, they even share an anecdote that makes everyone smile. My mother had laughed with the guards. She knew I was in a 'school,' but whenever she came to see me, their underhanded kindness fell like a veil over her eyes. She let herself be gulled by their hypocritical games. And so, despite my drawn features, the rings under my eyes that almost covered my entire cheek, my emaciated frame, she could never really imagine what I was going through. She didn't ask many questions. Whenever she ventured one, I'd give her an evasive reply. I didn't want her to know. I've said it before, and I'll say it again: in Xinjiang, knowing the truth puts you in danger.

When she arrived at the apartment, she remarked that I was 'not too battered' and even 'looking healthy.' And after that, she stood by it. Still, I could've called. 'Why didn't you come to see me?' she pressed with an incredulous air. She was upset. Worse yet, wounded. I sank into the sofa, devoured by guilt. Nedjma and Madina understood my shame and changed the subject, but my mother stubbornly persisted. 'You could have at least called! That wasn't very nice of you!'

They were well into their stay when the deal I'd made with the police came back to haunt me. The conversations took a schizophrenic turn. I wavered between feeling carefree and guilt-ridden. The real Gulbahar had vanished to make way for another, one walled in by lies. When my mother told me the latest from Kerim, Gulhumar, and Gulnigar, I took no real pleasure in it, for right away I recalled something the police had said: 'Tell your mother and sisters to pass this message on. It's very important. You were punished because Kerim and Gulhumar did something very bad. They took part in France Uyghur Association activities. That is why you were sent to school. She must also explain this to your husband and daughter.' The policeman became insistent. 'She must be very firm with Gulhumar and instruct her never to attend one of these protests again.'

When we called, Gulhumar happened to be with her family in Sweden. I asked my mother to repeat what the policemen had ordered me to tell her to say. She complied without batting an eye. I don't think it even crossed her mind that I could be in league with the police. She thought I was free, because nothing led her to suspect the contrary: here I was, living alone in a

Karamay apartment, seemingly accountable to no one apart from a few smiling neighbourhood committee members. I played my part in this subtle charade; it was terrifying. Inside, I was screaming.

The day came for them to leave, and when it did, my mother's incomprehension became ever more urgent. What was this? She couldn't stay? But that was insane! She stared at the three of us, eyes bright with worry. She wanted some real answers. All I had to give her was one more whopper the police had left me with. 'I'm sorry, Mama, but I have a lot of things to do here in Karamay. I have to find another apartment. I also have stop by the company to wrap up some paperwork. I'm really sorry, but you can't stay. Nedjma and Madina filled the suitcases. They took the long dresses down from their hangers, gathered the pairs of slippers by the door, wiped down the kitchen counters. They understood it was time to go. They knew that soon other people would be coming back into the apartment, the men or women keeping watch over me. The police. So they went about their business as I looked on, ashamed. Without a word, Nedjma packed away my mother's things. My mother was crying. 'I have no idea what's going on!' she sobbed. Once the apartment was empty, we slammed the door and rode to the airport. My mother cried the whole way, even when we were hugging each other goodbye, even as the escalator took her up into the crowd and out of my sight.

Afterwards, stretched out on my bed, I listened to the silence interrupted now and then by city noise: horns, engines revving. Distant voices chatting away in Mandarin. When the police saw my defeated expression on the way back from the airport, they gave in and granted me an extra reprieve. They left me alone that night. It was the first night I'd spent on my own in a very long time: without guards, fellow prisoners, Nedjma and Madina. Without my mother. Her sobs still echoed in my head, growing ever more distant as my body went numb.

26. Closing My File

The days stretched slowly out in the unrelenting summer heat. City-dwellers holed up in their air-conditioned homes. The departure of my mother and sisters had sent me spinning into the latest routine: grocery shopping, hair salon, restaurant, like the other residents of Karamay. But I didn't get a kick out of it anymore. This life of mine might have fooled old acquaintances who spotted me in the street, but not me. Cooking, cleaning, and shopping became excuses to kill time during my unbearable wait.

I didn't know what I was waiting for: a sign? Word from the police that would suddenly bring the end of all this into view. I lived on the alert. My ear was attuned to the policewomen's conversations, looking for who knew what: good news, bad news – any news, really. That was when they began almost feverishly talking about closing my 'file,' which led me to believe that I might soon be free. Way up there, far above the morose life the policemen and I shared, negotiations between France and China were at last taking a concrete turn, it seemed. 'It'll all be over soon, Gulbahar,' I was told. But as usual, nobody saw fit to tell me what this 'end' might consist of. Life in Xinjiang under police guard? Or a return to France? I didn't dare hope. Gulhumar's pregnancy was coming to term; the baby was due in early autumn, maybe before. In truth, I had a hard time keeping things straight because I was living in a parallel dimension in space-time. When would I be allowed to stop living a lie? Although the police often brought up my impending release, I was being kept in the dark, pitch blackness. All I could tell was that I was not yet free.

I'd been allowed to move into another apartment – my own, this time. I'd found a one-bedroom downtown, not without difficulty, since most landlords would no longer rent to Uyghurs. It was agreed that I'd sign the lease on 5th July. But that day, it all fell apart. As I was getting ready, anxious yet cheerful, for a taste of this new freedom, Madina called. My mother had just had a stroke. She was in a coma, hovering between life and death in the ICU at the hospital in Ghulja. My sister didn't say much more over the phone. She was packing her bags; she'd reach the hospital later that day. Nedjma and my brothers were already there. I gathered my things and, without waiting, bought a seat on the first flight to Ghulja. 'All right, you can go. But I'm coming with you,' Israyil immediately replied when I notified him of the situation. He booked the flight after mine. He would monitor my movements, spare me the agonising wait at security checkpoints, he said. He knew all about those. But he didn't fool me. He was crashing my trip to keep an eye on me, not to 'protect' me.

At the time, I didn't care if I was always going to be harassed by the police. In a way, my mother's stroke brought my house arrest in Karamay to a swifter end. Thanks to this unfortunate incident, I could pack my bags, hop on a flight – travel freely. I left with a heavy heart, guilt and sadness eating me up inside, my phone in my purse, always on so the police could reach me. I hoped I'd get there in time.

❄ ❄ ❄

Now I am at my mother's house. Eid al-Adha, the Festival of the Sacrifice, has just ended. The last few weeks in Ghulja have been strange. I am finally getting some rest and rediscovering the museum of my childhood, sometimes overcome by discomfiting nostalgia. I am heavy-hearted: no doubt because my brothers and sisters have all left the house. They're gone, and I'll never see them again. This much I know for certain. Our goodbyes were for good. The thought is so heartbreaking that it doesn't stir any feelings whatsoever, not yet. I let my gaze play over the finely crafted knick-knacks on the shelves, the Uyghur weavings on the walls, the rugs strewn across the floor.

My mother made it! She survived. After two weeks, her left foot twitched, then her hand. There'll be physical repercussions, but still, what a joy it was to see her coming out of the coma and back to herself, and to us, her children. Now she spends the better part of the day resting, a rest that Nedjma and I oversee. Since the festive days of Eid, nothing has disturbed the quietude of her recovery apart from my phone, which still rings several times a day. Its vibrations deep in my pocket remind me of my obligations. Israyil is trying to reach me. My release is imminent. It's a matter of days now, weeks at the most, and even as I try to picture the events that have brought me to this long-awaited moment, I'm not sure how I feel about it. The whirlwind of the crazed month of July flashes before my eyes with even greater clarity. With its contradictions, its doubts, its reprieves.

❀ ❀ ❀

In mid-July, my mother had been fighting for her life. Along with Nedjma, Madina, and the others, I spent my days at her bedside, watching over as she slept. I'd never thought to see my brothers again. But life's trials and tribulations can also bring us together. We'd pounced on the chance, spending our days supporting each other, telling each other about our lives by the water fountain, hugging each other as the nurses looked on discreetly, bustling from patient to patient. When we weren't trying to see my mother through the porthole of her sterilised room, our exhausted bodies sought rest against a wall. There, in the hallway, we slumped, let ourselves slip slowly down to the tile. The doctors tried to be optimistic. 'She'll come out of it,' they said, 'be patient.' Around us, men with a specific affliction dragged themselves around on crutches. I immediately recognised the disjointed way these rickety patients moved, with their pale skin and sunken eyes, as if they'd been deprived of natural light for a long time. It's what years in a camp does to you. When you've been shackled together for days or even weeks, your tibia atrophies, your ankles swell, your feet grow twisted. Some of these zombies were even wearing blue uniforms. My theory was soon confirmed. After observing one of them for several days – a man of about 50 – I finally struck up a conversation with him. 'Yes, I just got out of a school,' he acknowledged in a whisper. 'There are a lot of us here.'

Meanwhile, Israyil had checked into a hotel in Ghulja. From one of the benches in the hospital garden, he kept up his daily surveillance. I split my time between the hallway and that bench, between my siblings, who had no idea he was here, and my meetings with him, which he would initiate with a phone call. That was the summons: the minute I saw his number on my screen, I had to dash off to the garden. The same schizophrenia that had driven me to lie when my mother and sisters had visited Karamay now took hold of my hospital days: he called, I came running.

His generosity towards me astonished me. The more my case 'moved forward,' the more solicitude he showed me, and the border between our two worlds crumbled. As if, suddenly, I were no longer a terrorist in his eyes, but a person to be protected. An individual to be kept under watch but also watched over, cared for, because he cared about me. I realised then that in a policeman's mind, only the thinnest of lines divides these two categories. Through the magic of negotiations taking place in hushed offices thousands of miles away, the little kindnesses he showed me multiplied. My sworn enemy, the final link in the chain of my tormentors, now concerned himself with my deepest personal worries. His connections made the crisis we were going through easier. He'd notified the police in Ghulja of my mother's stroke, and they had rushed to meet with hospital management to make sure she was looked after by the finest doctors. I'd update him with the latest on her condition, and in return, he would pass me messages from Kerim and Gulhumar, who agonised knowing I was at my dying mother's bedside. He'd reassure them over the phone, saying: 'Patience. Just a little bit longer.' I watched as he handled my case all the way to the end, anxious to make sure I'd soon be free. It's very strange to say, but in his fretful gaze I no longer read anything but kindness. A sincere attentiveness and consideration I simply could not wrap my head around after everything people like him had put me through.

The stinging fluorescence that blinded you, the lessons, the meals, the forced processions both identical and endless – in the camps, these were powerful ways of torturing you that made you lose all sense of time. For two years, I'd languished in the limbo of days in detention where nothing and no one awaited you. I'd forgotten that hours were ticking by, days and months slipping away. On the outside, my case had been passed from one hand to another so many times that I'd stopped hoping it would ever be resolved. For it, too, time seemed to have halted, suspended as the Karamay police station busied itself with protocol, hectic as an anthill.

And then, all of a sudden, though I had no idea why, time sped up. After so much time spent without any notion of time, the police were hurrying me around. First I was placed in house arrest for a few months. Then on parole during my mother's convalescence. When she was discharged from the hospital and Israyil summoned me to his hotel room four days later, I realised that the time until my release was a matter of days. The more I cooperated, the faster my case would be closed. I went from a hollowed, shattered life on the margins where death seemed the only likely end that awaited, to a life of rushing and pressure. I was running a marathon of bureaucratic paperwork that would allow me to return to France.

In his hotel room, flanked by several other officers I didn't recognise, Israyil asked me to write out new confessions. Again? Would this song and dance never end? There was already the video they'd shot in March, but they needed an 'official written apology,' he said. I did as I was told, and before one of the policemen seized my confession and added it to my file, I saw him date the document 11th March, 2019, the date my house arrest was lifted. I found that strange. Even now, that detail remains a mystery to me. But as before, the police left me no time to ponder it. They were tasked with closing my case and taking me back to Karamay. I said goodbye to my family, promising to come back in early August for Eid.

It was late July. When we landed Karamay was snoozing in a heatwave. The next few days were unreal. No sooner had we reached the apartment than the police ordered me to pack my bags. I was moved to a hotel room downtown. I never even bothered to put away my hastily balled-up clothes, leaving them where my suitcase had vomited them at the foot of the bed. I slept so little I barely mussed the sheets. I knew that I wouldn't be here long. It was a sure thing now that Tasqin was intending to take me to the passport office. He announced this in utterly neutral tones, as if there were nothing extraordinary about such a petty formality. My heart began beating fit to burst, the very thought of it ricocheting around inside my head: I was getting a passport! In just a few weeks, I'd be able to leave this country! Apparently, I needed a new one. Tasqin would personally see to it that I could obtain one 'without delay' by 'reaching out to his network,' he assured me. His high status would help me wend my way more quickly through the tortuous maze of endless protocol in Xinjiang. I couldn't get over it. In a few days, every door in this intricate, perplexing administration had opened for me with unsettling ease. The man at the service window even wondered: what was the exact date I wished to return to France? I was being asked for my opinion. Another man asked when Gulhumar was due: as first-time mothers often gave birth early, I had to be there 'well in advance,' he recommended. 'The passport office will take care of everything,' he added gently. My God: I was going home. Who were these powers on high seeing to my release and – I could barely say the words out loud – my return home? Was it Gulhumar and Kerim? France? France! It was happening! I was going back to France.

For two years, everyone around me – police officers, guards, professors, tutoresses – had tried to make me swallow the massive lie with which China justified its 're-education' project: all Uyghurs were terrorists. I, Gulbahar, was a Uyghur living in exile in France. Therefore, I was a terrorist. The endless waves of propaganda crashed down upon me, and as the months went by, I lost part of my mind. First in jail, and then in the camp, my soul splintered and fragments drifted off, never to be seen again.

I caved into police violence, knuckled under. I even signed a false confession, I was told that the sooner I acknowledged my crimes, the sooner I'd be let out. Worn down, I finally believed them. I accepted my role, for in the oblivion of the camps, no other choice was available. You can't fight off brainwashing forever, even if you think you can. Once you've fought it with dignity, it sets to work. All desire and willpower desert you. What options do you have left then? A slow, excruciating slide toward death or... submission. But if you play at submission, if you feign giving into the power struggle the police are waging, then you can hold onto a shard of lucidity that reminds you who you are. They believed I was sincere in my repentance. Me, I never believed a single word of what I was made to say. I was just a good actress. I want to go on the record with that now, since the police are such experts at manipulation. All around me, I saw detainees succumb right and left.

By warping my mind in this way, I was able to make myself an invincible shield. I never forgot the truth. I am innocent. When Ayshem asserted how much I'd harmed China, I nodded. Deep down, even in my most intense moments of despair, I knew. Not that my innocence would triumph, since I was one among thousands of targets of a massive plot meant to wipe out all Uyghurs, but that my innocence could never be taken away from me. Not by Ayshem, not by the police; no one could keep me from believing that till the day I died.

Shortly before noon on 2nd August, a judge in Karamay pronounced me innocent before a tiny gathering. After the recent set of confessions and the passport application, here was the final stage in my release: a trial. A real trial. To tell the truth, I didn't catch what he said, because I wasn't really listening. I was there, but looking on, almost like a stranger. My camp number was read aloud, as were the charges against me, and then it was like I flew away. I wasn't there anymore. I was floating weightlessly above them in a comatose reverie. I thought back to all those times I'd protested my innocence, the nights spent tossing and turning on my straw mattress, enraged there was not a soul around who believed me. And then I thought back to all those other times as well: the times I'd bowed before their accusations, the ones I'd confessed to. All those loudly proclaimed lies.

Around me, the policemen were stirring. 'Did you hear that? The judge just set you free. You've done it, you're free!' one of them whispered. I looked at him, unable to smile back. I'd been sentenced to seven years of 're-education': they'd dragged my body through hell and my mind to the brink of madness. And now, after three years of looking into my case, the police had submitted their conclusions: after reading my file over closely, a judge decreed that no, actually I was innocent! Acknowledged after a delay (three years!) I could never forgive, the contempt with which they'd treated me only made everything more absurd. Who were all these psychopaths telling me one day that I had to pay for my 'crimes' with seven years in a concentration camp, and the next, freeing me with something akin to boredom? I hadn't heard any apologies, or mention of any reparation whatsoever for the three years of my life that had been stolen from me, three years in which I'd been reduced to something less than a woman. I hadn't heard even a whisper of that. The judge gathered his papers, and then everyone in the room began to rise. There was a scraping of benches being pushed back. It was over. That is how my torment came to an end: in indifference.

I remained seated amid the havoc, stunned by the news. The verdict put an end to my parole. I was truly free. At last.

My passport was due to arrive any day now. Every time Israyil or Tasqin called, I hoped they had news about it. I pounced on messages from unlisted numbers on my phone. My entire being should have been filled with intense happiness. And yet, the complete opposite was the case. I couldn't bring myself to face the fact that soon I'd have to say goodbye to my mother, to my sisters, to my country. I would never return. My mother was dozing, eyelids a-flutter, in her bedroom. When I looked at her, I saw a great sadness in her face, lined with anxious wrinkles. She knew it too: in a few days, all this would be over. We would never see each other ever again. I was leaving tomorrow to see Kerim's family for a few days in Altay, the first time I'd seen my in-laws since I was arrested in January 2017. Then I'd come back here to bid my mother and Nedjma farewell. Then it was off to Ürümqi. There I'd get my ticket for France and Madina would see me to the airport. We'd give each other a great big hug. And that would be the last I'd ever see of Xinjiang.

27. Landing

21st August 2019

5.40pm. Just another 15 minutes and I'd be with them. 'Ladies and gentlemen, we are now starting our final descent. Passengers, please return to your seats and make sure your seatbelts are securely fastened.' Around me, people quietly readied themselves. The rustle of newspapers being tucked away and the click of tray tables being folded into seat backs mingled with the buckling of seatbelts. I watched the dark mass of woods outside the window, the line of road as it snaked through the pretty yellow-and-green palette of the fields from above, the tiny cars.

I clutched the plastic cup a flight attendant had handed me earlier A few drops of water still clung to its sides. Here I was. It was all over now. Funny, I'd imagined I'd be flooded with immense relief at this moment. The plane dipped and, as the blood beat in my temples from the pressure, I surrendered to the few minutes that still divided me from France – from Kerim, Gulhumar, and Gulnigar. Last night, I'd chewed over what to say, what not to. I looked at my story from every angle in my head, keeping myself awake. I checked my watch. 5.42pm. What would we say to each other. When we saw each other, who would speak first? Would I faint? Maybe the best solution was to pretend. I hoped Kerim would relax the atmosphere. He always was good at that. Yes, we should all probably pretend this was just another homecoming like any other. That all the suffering had just been a nightmare. One of those nightmares that leave you paralysed in the sheets upon waking, throat tight, even though you can't quite remember what had terrified you in your sleep.

If I hugged them, I would start crying. That much was certain. I didn't want to cry. A little dignity, please. We would unburden ourselves later, away from prying gazes.

A flight attendant made her way down the rows, checking seatbelts. I eyed the second hand moseying around my watch face. How slow it was! I felt pins and needles all over my body. What would they think of me? I ran a shaky hand through my lank hair, and then over the small brown marks on my cheek. Snap out of it, Gulbahar, they won't be thinking anything at all. They'll just be happy to see you. 5.43pm. This was taking forever. Gulhumar had explained everything on the phone. She and the Foreign Ministry had planned my return down to the very last detail so that nothing bad could happen to me. In Astana, the French Embassy in Kazakhstan had sent a woman to watch over me while I was waiting to change planes. I never saw her, but she was there, somewhere in the crowd of passengers in the terminal.

We might even have exchanged glances.

Once my flight had taken off from Kazakhstan, I felt an initial wave of relief. Still, so long as I wasn't back with my family, I was not yet free. Not entirely. Once again, I leaned forward to study the other passengers, seeking one of Tasqin's henchmen. Maybe he'd had me followed to France. Maybe someone would get up all of a sudden, walk over to me, and say: 'Gulbahar Haitiwaji? Come with me, please. We have a few more questions.' The possibility obsessed me. I gripped the armrests and stretched out my neck for a better look. In front. In back. No, no one was giving me suspicious glances. No one seemed to recognise me. There were only people dozing and others slowly waking up. 5.45pm. I sank back into my seat.

They'd find me changed, that much was certain. When I'd bid goodbye to my mother in her home and Madina at the airport, I'd left a piece of myself in their arms. Part of my soul, too, was still wandering the cold hallways at Baijiantan, sitting in the courtroom where the policeman who judged me was no doubt passing sentence on other innocent people. Nothing would ever be the same again. The madness sweeping our planet had forever torn me from the peaceful life I once lived. My family wouldn't recognise me because I wasn't the same person anymore. Those unspeakable things – prisoners hollowed-out shells of themselves, police galvanised by propaganda, all those people reduced to less than human beings by the brutal shock of repression – how could I ever forget them?

An abrupt jolt brought me back to the here and now of the cabin. 5.56pm. We'd just landed. Outside the window, the runway at Roissy was bathed in golden light. The flight attendant addressed us in Mandarin, then French. I swallowed and rubbed my damp palms on my pants. Once we'd gotten over the reunion, what then? How would we pick it up again? 'Three years ago, I was thrown in jail....' No, that wouldn't work. 'They put me in a 're-education' camp.' No, that wouldn't work either. Too cold, too hard. 'Do you want me to tell you what happened to me?' Yes, maybe that was a way I could begin my story.

But for now, there was nothing else to be said. Nothing else to be done. Not a thought in my head but their beloved faces waiting for me a stone's throw away, at the other end of the passage connecting the plane to the airport. I fell in line with the passengers quietly hurrying on their way. I felt like running.

Afterword by Rozenn Morgat

January 2021

Whenever a silence lasts a few seconds too long, that's the usual alarm signal, the secret code that lets Gulbahar know the FaceTime conversation she's having with her mother and sisters will soon be cut short. 'Well, um, guess I better be running along now,' one of the women will say with some awkwardness. Curled up on the white sofa in Boulogne with her grandson Rafael on her knees, Gulbahar will nod. Her body tenses as she straightens up on the cushions. For just one minute more, she takes in their dear faces on-screen, then sees them off with a wave from Rafael's pudgy little hand. 'Bye bye, see you next week!' Rafael gurgles, and it does her heart good to hear it.

Her mother, Nedjma and Madina are doing fine. Or at any rate that's what they say whenever Gulbahar calls, which happens once a week since returning to France. Of course, the conversations never last long. If they ever did drag on, the women might run out of topics to discuss. As before, in Karamay, there are things they don't talk about. They can't admit that police interrogations in Xinjiang are multiplying, and that many people around them keep getting sent to the camps. When Gulbahar learns that one of her nephews needs crutches now, or another is in poor health, she understands what is meant. She knows how to interpret these coded messages. She's learned to surmise what they are forced to leave out of their conversations, doubtless monitored. So all four women make do with small talk. Bringing up trifles from their lives.

Gulbahar closes up her phone case, gives Rafael a big loud smooch, and sits him down on his playmat. She goes about her business. On weekends, Kerim, Gulhumar, and Gulnigar also attend to their affairs in the apartment during the downtime after lunch when every room dozes in a bluish light. Keeping herself busy at home helps her think, even if her whole body suddenly feels sapped of strength at times. Poor sleep from short, restless nights keeps her in a state of constant, nagging fatigue. Her vision has also deteriorated badly and violent headaches sometimes prevent her from finishing her sentences. Those damned blinding lights in Baijiantan. For a few weeks now, a question has obsessed her: what will become of her mother and sisters when the Chinese authorities learn of this book? She checks WeChat on her phone with a worried eye, then sends a few messages to Madina and Nedjma. 'I hope everything's OK. I'll call you really soon.' Free though she may be, Gulbahar still lives with the fear, vast and uncontrollable, that one day she'll call and there'll be no answer. Just thinking about it knots her stomach.

And Aynur? What of her? And Dilnur, Almira, Zahida, all the other women she met in the camps – what became of them? Gulbahar takes a deep dive into videos posted by people she knows on WeChat and TikTok, an investigation that leads nowhere. It's as if these women have vanished from the face of the earth. One day, Gulbahar chanced upon a trace of one of them, a fellow detainee at Baijiantan, of Kazakh descent. 'Hello! How are you? I'm Prisoner No. 9,' she wrote. The other woman never responded. Now that she's on the other side of the looking glass, Gulbahar looks on, terrified as Xinjiang becomes more closed-off than ever, a black hole sucking in everyone she's ever loved, whom she could contact before the tragedy that befell her. To reassure herself, she remembers the precious number the French Foreign Ministry gave her two months after she came back. 'If there's anything you need, if you feel threatened or in danger, call us,' they'd told her at the time. Gulbahar hasn't forgotten. If her messages to her mother, Nedjma, or Madina go unanswered, she won't think twice about dialling that number.

Today, Gulbahar no longer fears for her life. When she goes out grocery shopping, she'll look over her shoulder now and then to make sure she's not being followed – an old reflex – but she has received no threats or attempts at blackmail. For now at least, no shadow has fallen over the peaceful daily life she leads with her family. She has found her place again in Boulogne, filled the gaping hole her disappearance left behind, and more. Now Gulbahar, once a self-effacing woman who steered clear of the heated debates over Xinjiang, makes it her business not only to make sure that her loved ones lack for nothing, but also to listen.

When discussion at the dinner table drifts toward politics, she has things to say. She sets a platter of *laghman* down among the dishes and recounts what she witnessed in Xinjiang. Everyone listens to her in silence. A hint of pride gleams in Kerim's eye; the repression has been a source of disgust for so many years now. Gulbahar grows used to this new role with delight, like a free woman, determined to turn her trauma and her wounds into strength.

And yet, she never imagined that freedom would taste so bitter. When she'd given up, wasting away in a camp, nothing seemed happier than coming back to France. She'd visualised the reunion at the airport, the hugs, the tears, her daughters in her arms, everyone shaking with sobs. A few weeks after that happened, Gulbahar got back in touch with her diaspora friends. They'd all followed her ordeal through Gulhumar's petitions and interviews. Some came and gave her daughter gifts after Rafael was born. Others wrote her letters. That was when she realised something was wrong. That was when she realised, distraught, that China had won.

The repression in Xinjiang made itself felt in the small community of Uyghurs in France, to such an extent that the outpouring of warmth from her friends was not as great as she'd hoped. Gulbahar was welcomed back only tepidly, even coldly. On their worried faces, in the text messages they left answered, she saw something like discomfort, a barely perceptible fear. 'It's not that I don't want to see you, you know. But I feel uneasy. Your apartment must be bugged,' a very close friend finally confessed. Rumours about the Haitiwajis abounded: how was it that

Gulbahar had been freed? No one ever got out of those camps. Had she made a deal with the police? Had she named names? No matter which way you cut it, there was something odd about her release. She must have collaborated with them. That was what people were saying. In the empty moments of embarrassed silence, she realised that she was no longer seen as a victim, but rather a spy. A traitor in the fold, among her own kind.

The situation in China did her no favours: the more they steamrollered over everything there, the more paranoid the people of the diaspora became. Rather than slowing down, China stepped up its massive 're-education' project in Xinjiang. Outside its borders, the country kept right on scheming to silence any voices likely to thwart its plans. So it was that in April 2020, the credibility of the UN Human Rights Council suffered a remarkable blow when a Chinese official, Jiang Duan, was appointed to serve on a Consultative Group representing the Asia-Pacific States, one of five regional groups on the panel. Another followed that October, when China was among the member states elected to the Council for a three-year term. Meanwhile, revelations were surfacing left and right, denouncing the forced labour of Uyghur prisoners in factories subcontracted to 'at least 82' globally recognised brands. The United States and Europe requested that international delegations finally be given access to Xinjiang. But China ignored or refused. Now China, that gruesome world leader in capital punishment – China, which imprisons its Uyghurs in camps, brainwashes them, subjects them to torture and forced labour – is one of the nations that will be making the rules on human rights.

Sickened by all this, wounded, but patient, Gulbahar has nevertheless made her peace with her friends' mistrust. 'If that's the price to pay to be alive and free...' she says. Her resilience, the very resilience that kept her from going under in the camps, comes to her aid now when she realises almost nostalgically that her life these days no longer has anything in common with her life from before. She will never be the same Gulbahar. Memories of the camps keep surfacing from her fractured recollections. These still pervade her entire body and soul. She will never be embarrassed by the fact of being freed. And if one day, those now keeping their distance from her ever ask what happened in Xinjiang, she will tell them of the chaos that gradually took over her soul over the course of her interrogations. The lassitude that filled every corner of her being as she was brainwashed. Her failing memory. The way you become a stranger to yourself. The fear and anguish of nights in the dark pierced by women's screams in the distance. The slamming of cell doors drowning out the stifled sobs. Friends who became victims of the police. She will tell them that, just like Rebiya Kadeer, she was forced to confess in front of a camera. And that one day, to discredit her, authorities in Xinjiang will surely disseminate this video on social media. She will, without a second thought, forgive her friends for doubting her, for she knows that in its zeal for repression, China spares not a single Uyghur.

Acknowledgements

This book owes a great deal to Gulbahar's daughter Gulhumar, who never, in the two and a half years her mother was imprisoned, gave up the fight to free her from the Chinese gulag. She is the secret heroine of this story, a liaison between Gulbahar and myself, acting as a meticulous interpreter during all our conversations on that white sofa in Boulogne.

For her priceless eye as well as her advice, my thanks to Jeanne Pham Tran, our editor at Editions des Equateurs, who has been keeping abreast of the Uyghur situation for years.

For their support, advice, and shrewd, enthusiastic readings of this manuscript, my thanks – last but not least – to my family, as well as Delphine, Mehdi, Romain, and Xavier.

Rozenn Morgat

See the world more clearly. All year round.

We're committed to finding talented writers and getting their books into the hands of the right people: people like you. If you'd like to be updated on our new projects, please sign up to our email newsletter at www.canburypress.com – you'll get 10 per cent off all titles you order from our website – or consider our new subscription service.

By subscribing, you allow us to invest in important new non-fiction. For £70 for 12 months, you'll receive:

- Five new books, tailored to you
- With a total recommended retail price of at least £80
- Delivered pre-publication with free P&P
- At least one signed or special edition, or a free gift
- Advance notice and priority booking for author events.

Don't worry – we'll never send you a book you've already ordered from us. To join or gift a subscription, visit: www.canburypress.com/subscriptions

Due to the high cost of postage, this offer is available to UK residents only.